The Future
QUIXTAR
Consumer

THE PROSUMER WEBOLUTION:
Changing Everyday Shopping Habits
to Build a Home-Based e-Business

~ 2004 EDITION ~

Frank Feather

author of
Future Consumer.Com
and
Future Living

The Future QUIXTAR Consumer
2004 Edition

To Contact Frank Feather:

• **Suggestions and/or Questions:** To submit ideas on how to
enhance the value of this book, please e-mail your suggestions
and/or questions to FutureTrends2020@aol.com

• **Speaking Engagements:** To reserve Frank Feather to speak
to your organization, please telephone or e-mail him directly
at (905) 642-9090 or FutureTrends2020@aol.com

• **Website:** Visit www.Future-Trends.com

To Re-Order This Book:
See the **Order Form** at the back of the book.

For Bulk Discount Pricing:

John Cordova, National Sales Manager
Inspire Media LLC
4621 Delafield Drive
La Mirada, CA 90638

Tel: (702) 493-1789 ; Fax : (714) 844-4858
E-Mail: john@inspiremedia.biz

ISBN: 0-9689763-4-4
2004 Edition, Published January 2004
Printed in U.S.A.

WHAT PEOPLE SAY ABOUT THIS BOOK

(Abstracts from Reviews posted at Amazon.com)

• SUPER!! GIVES YOU a "HEAD START" on YOUR QUIXTAR BUSINESS
(Debbie Cana, Quixtar IBO, Dallas, Texas)

Super book! We use it as a "first night" tool that we lend out. We have 8 copies in constant circulation! Registrations are growing nearly 3 times faster and our team's PV/BV is growing rapidly. It's like having Frank Feather as your private consultant, right there alongside you, presenting the plan. It's magical!

• A GREAT THIRD-PARTY OPINION of the QUIXTAR BUSINESS MODEL!
(Quixtar IBO in San Francisco, California)

Compelling! An absolute "must have"! Full of honest and professional data ... serious Team Builders will want 5-10 copies to let Frank Feather "go to work" for them through his book. It's a wonderful learning tool for IBOs to understand what a powerful business they have their hands on – and to teach the same.

• CONTINUE YOUR QUIXTAR ADVENTURE
(Giovanni Zappetta, Quixtar IBO, Vacaville, California)

A definite asset in building a Quixtar business. Those wanting first mover advantage need the right tools – and this is definitely one of them. Full of facts and fun to read, it just flows. You won't put it down because you'll want to know what's on the next page, the next chapter – heck, the next book!

• LOOKING for an INTERNET OPPORTUNITY? READ THIS!
(Quixtar IBO in Toronto, Canada)

For those who want to know where e-commerce is going, Frank Feather's credentials are impeccable. This is an excellent resource for IBOs – one of the best contacting tools available – or for anyone thinking about a Quixtar business.

• CREATE MORE REGISTRATIONS!!
(Quixtar IBO in Corona, California)

Want more registrations? This book will do just that! We found if you hand out 3 to 5 books to potential IBOs the registration rate increases. This book will give you truth about what's happening in the industry. I highly recommend this book to add credibility to your organization. I wish I'd had it sooner!

• MUST READ for ALL QUIXTAR IBOs
(Chuck Addison, San Jose, CA)

Works wonders when presenting the plan; lends instant credibility. It's full of facts to bolster your presentation and answer questions. Feather's impartial opinion is invaluable. He concludes that Quixtar could become the SUN of the entire e-shopping universe! And once you've read this book you will see why.

DEDICATED TO

Those with the Motivation
to
Embrace the "Webolution"
and
Change their Shopping Habits
by
Starting a Family e-Business
@
Quixtar.com

THIS BOOK BELONGS TO

_____

_____

_____
_____
(Please Return It – Thank You!)

CONTENTS

ABOUT THIS BOOK
and
HOW TO USE IT

T HIS IS A VERY DIFFERENT BOOK. It is a Quixtar-specific book about online shopping trends, about the ongoing Quixtar success story, and the strategic implications for building a Quixtar business.

A third-party "outsider" to Quixtar, I've written this book as an objective look at Quixtar-relevant facts, trends and ideas — all revised and updated for 2004.

Written Especially for 3 Groups of People

It's a tightly-focused, user-friendly, quick study, especially written for 3 types of readers:

- • Potential Quixtar Online Shoppers
- • Prospective Quixtar IBOs
- • Existing Quixtar IBO e-Business Builders

This Book has 3 Goals

1. **PAINT THE "BIG PICTURE"** of the technical, economic, social, and shopping "webolutions" to the extent that they impact Quixtar;

2. **EXPLAIN WHY QUIXTAR** already is and will continue to be a top online place to shop and, hence, why it is the *best* e-business opportunity;

3. **OFFER STRATEGIES AND IDEAS** on building a turnkey e-business success with Quixtar.

Organized in 3 Logical Parts

PART I: THE "BIG PICTURE" WEBOLUTION

Chapters 1, 2, and 3 describe the technological, economic, and social shifts caused by the Internet Revolution or "Webolution."

PART II: THE QUIXTAR SHOPPER

Chapter 4 draws on the first three chapters to forecast how much shopping will be done online as the Webolution unfolds.

Chapter 5 describes, analyzes, and forecasts the behavior and buying habits of tomorrow's best Quixtar shopping prospects.

PART III: THE QUIXTAR BUSINESS

Chapter 6 describes the Quixtar success story to date and predicts Quixtar's future chances as the Webolution of shopping continues.

Chapter 7 concludes the book with strategies and ideas on how to build a successful online Quixtar business.

Note: For full discussions of the shopping "webolution" and "web lifestyle" concepts used in this book, please refer to: *Future Consumer.Com* (updated 2002 soft cover); *Future Living* (2003); *Get a Web Life* (2004).

How to Use This Book

Since this book first came out in 2002, tens of thousands of copies have been put to use by Quixtar IBOs, either as a business-building tool or as a teaching and coaching tool.

1. As a Business-Building Tool

At Quixtar events where I speak, and via unsolicited but welcome e-mails, scores of IBOs have told me they're using this book to great success in growing their business. They use the following simple 2-step process:

STEP 1: LEND OUT MULTIPLE COPIES

IBOs are investing in multiple copies of the book (buying 3, 5, even 10 copies – *see Note* below*) and lending them to new prospects during the *first* presentation of the Quixtar opportunity.

IBOs call it a "First Night" book that validates Quixtar's business model.

The book allows people to see for themselves – through the impartial words of an "outsider" – the clear benefits of shopping online at Quixtar and/or of building a turnkey, home-based business of their own with Quixtar.

*(Note: For bulk copy purchase discounts, please contact the publisher – see inside front cover.)

STEP 2: PICK UP THE BOOK and RE-LEND IT

IBOs also schedule an appointment to pick up the book at a *"follow-up"* meeting – and then lend it out again to another prospect, repeating the cycle.

Some IBOs also say they are lending the book to people who previously were undecided about the Quixtar opportunity – or outright said "No" – and the book has convinced many of them to register.

With this 2-step process, IBOs say their **registration rate climbs** – putting their business on a fast-track growth path – and that their *new* IBOs are much happier with their own business start-up progress.

Many new IBOs confirm this, telling me that indeed this book convinced them to register! They also say the book helps them successfully present the business to others.

In sum, new IBOs say this book gives them a "head start" in launching their own business.

2. As a Primary Teaching and Coaching Tool

Quixtar organizations are adopting this book for teaching and coaching, using some or all of the following methods.

- **"Book of the Month"** – some organizations designate it as a book-of-the-month selection.

- **Review Meetings** – A senior IBO studies the book in depth and then leads a series of group discussions about the book – and how to make best use of it – at IBO meetings.

- **Mini Seminars** – Some IBOs teach internal "mini seminars" based on the book.

Why I Wrote This Book

A former bank executive, I've been a business strategy and marketing consultant since 1981, now specializing in e-commerce.

For me, it's easy to see why Quixtar is so successful. I am genuinely enthused about its future.

Even prior to Quixtar's launch in 1999, I believed Quixtar would be a big online winner. Since then, I have learned much more about Quixtar's unique "I-commerce" model, and I remain totally convinced of that prospect.

Simply put, Quixtar is in perfect alignment with business marketing and Internet trends.

That's because I believe the future of marketing and sales will be based on these 3 brand-new elements:

- **Affiliate marketing and online shopping**
- **One-to-one (1:1) "prosumer" relationships**
- **Turnkey "private franchise" businesses**

Quixtar epitomizes this e-business model! And that's really why I wanted to write this book about the Quixtar business opportunity – and to update it again for 2004.

I hope you find this book both useful and objective. I firmly believe it will help *you* build *your* Quixtar business – and I wish you every possible webolutionary success!

Frank Feather
January 2004

The Future QUIXTAR Consumer

Part I

THE "BIG PICTURE" of the WEBOLUTION

QUIXTAR WAS DESTINED TO BE BIG. But to put the immense Quixtar e-commerce opportunity in context, we need to understand the Internet Revolution (or "Webolution") and its impact on technology, the economy, and society. We'll do that in 3 separate chapters.

It is important to understand the "big picture" context of the future before forecasting online shopping – and the huge opportunity it represents for Quixtar.

The operative word here is "big." So please do not skip this section or you will not grasp the magnitude of what's happening – never mind the exciting prospects within your reach.

The Future QUIXTAR Consumer

1

THE TECHNOLOGY WEBOLUTION

The Coming Wireless Web

A BRAND-NEW PC is switched on for the first time in human history every second, 24 hours a day, non-stop, globally.

If that astonishing fact doesn't send shivers down your spine, then you don't "get it." But if that excites you, then you too need to tap into the "shopping webolution." And don't take my word for it. Read this:

> *"Virtually everything that was discussed about the Internet – even the most hyped thing – will happen. It just takes a bit more time."*
>
> – Bill Gates, July 2003, at the
> Microsoft Research Faculty Summit

Internet Explosion: 1 Billion Online!

The Web is exploding. In 1993, there were only 5,000 computers connected to the Internet. **At last count, 670 million
people worldwide are online.** By the end of 2005, there
will be 1 billion online – mostly via cell phone!

In fact, there are now twice as many cell phones
sold every year as PCs and 1.2 billion are in use globally.
The newest phones are permanently connected to the Web
and by 2008 there will be 2 billion cell phones, most of
them permanently-online WebPhones.

As a result, the Internet has spread across society
and into our lives faster than any previous medium. To
reach a critical mass of 50 million North American users,
radio took 38 years, TV 13 years, PCs 8 years, and the Web
only 5 years. Moreover, Web use is growing five times
faster than TV and ten times faster than radio.

Today, 70% of North American homes already use
the Web regularly, many of them for several hours a day.
Next year, 2005, Web usage will surpass TV watching.

Hello!

**And since 98% of homes have radios, TVs, and
phones, it's fairly certain that 98% will be online by
2010. The Web will be a daily fact of life.**

Not long ago, as with every new technology, the
Internet brought out skeptics who said: "It will never work"
or "Nobody needs it." Well, nobody watched TV when it
first came out. And people wondered why anybody would
ever want a phone in their car.

In fact, the telephone, TV, and computers were all
summarily dismissed as being useless:

- **This "telephone" has too many shortcomings to be seriously considered as a means of communication. The device is inherently of no value to us.**
  — Western Union internal memo, 1876

- **Television will *never* be a serious competitor for radio because people must sit and keep their eyes glued on a screen; the average family hasn't time for it.**
  — New York Times article, 1939

- **There is no reason for *anybody* to have a computer in the home.**
  — Chairman, DEC computer company, 1977

In 1995, experts predicted that the Internet would collapse within a year because it wouldn't be able to handle the volume. Tell that to the 670 million online!

When a radically-new technology upsets the *status quo*, most people either dismiss it or take a wait-and-see attitude. After the initial hype, they become skeptical. But then realization dawns that *"Hey, this is for real!"*

Upon wider acceptance, there comes a flash point when much of the marketplace quickly shifts from the old to the new, and the technology takes off.

With the Internet, we are fast approaching what computer scientists call an "inflection point" where networked information will become instantaneously available to a "critical mass" of people.

As this occurs globally, around 2005, the Web will have become an everyday fact of life for the majority of people in North America, Western Europe, Australasia, Japan, South Korea, and other parts of Asia.

Internet Hype to Maturity Cycle

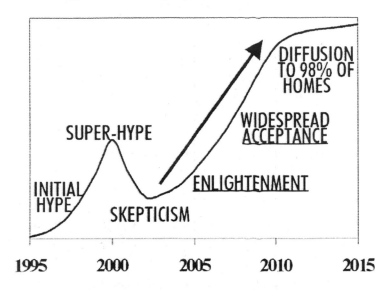

More than 75% of North American households already have a PC and 90% of those homes are online. Most of them are still learning the benefits of the Web and online shopping. And few people could yet claim to truly live a "Web Lifestyle." But that will happen as more people gain more online experience.

Once consumers go online, they never look back. Meanwhile, the Web is quietly changing consumer behavior, laying the groundwork for a widespread Web Lifestyle and an explosion of online shopping.

The "Network Effect" of Value Creation

The rapid growth of the Internet is due to its self-feeding "network effect."

The Web's network effect is similar in scale and scope to that of water, electricity, railway, airline, and highway networks. The more people connect to such networks, the better they function and the more efficient they become. They become more valuable to their users.

Networks must be of a certain size to function. Thus, if there is only one airport, airplanes have no place to go. But the more airports there are, the more valuable the air network becomes to its potential passengers, and more people see the advantages of using it. Its value literally takes off.

Centers of commerce always spring up around networks. This was the case with commodity exchanges, seaports, railroad stations, highway systems, airports, financial centers and malls.

> **The ongoing plunge in computing costs will revolutionize all of life and commerce.**
>
> **It underpins the entire e-commerce opportunity.**

Like the seaports and railroad towns of old, digital communities will flourish wherever there is money to be made from flowing bits – that is, on the Web.

In turn, the exponential growth in customer activity – not just of the network itself – expands the value of the network at lower incremental cost.

The larger the network, the greater is its value and wealth-creating potential.

The cost of computer processing has plunged more rapidly than any other technology in history. Since 1984, the inflation-adjusted cost of PCs has dropped almost 30% a year. That's astonishing!

This ongoing plunge in computing costs will revolutionize all of life and commerce. It underpins the entire e-commerce opportunity.

These computer productivity gains follow Moore's Law, named after Gordon Moore, the co-founder of Intel, the world's leading microchip maker. Back in the late-1960s, Moore astutely predicted that the processing power of chips (which did not come to market until 1971) would double every 18 months at the same price point or less.

This pattern has held since 1971 and Moore believes the trend will continue for at least another decade.

Wireless Web of Mobile Commerce

Looking ahead, the future of the Web is wireless. There is a brand new cell phone activated for the first time in history every half-second; every day 150,000 people buy a Web-ready cell phone. Close to 50% of cell phones now have Web browsing ability. That's about the same percentage as the number of PCs that had Web access in 1999.

In North America, cell phones already comprise 43% of all phones in use. They're so popular that phone companies are ripping out payphones. Some 28% of them have vanished in the U.S. in the last 6 years and the number of calls made on payphones is down 42%.

Even desk phones in offices are falling into disuse and will vanish from cubicles as people prefer to use their cell phone, pager, or PDA.

About 10 million North Americans have "cut the cord" and gone solo with their cell at home. Loving the cell phone's convenience, they also want a mobile Web.

Shopping will be a big part of the mobile Web, bringing m-commerce (mobile commerce) to the mass public.

For example, you could be in a taxi with a friend who tells you about the latest electronic book she's reading and immediately download it for yourself.

Alternatively, while visiting a brick-and-mortar store you can scan product bar codes to make price comparisons.

Then you could decide whether to buy on the spot or simply hit one button to instantly order and pay for the product online – from any e-tailer you chose – for automatic home delivery.

Handy-Dandy e-Shopping WebPhones

WebPhones will not only transplant PCs as the dominant Web access tool. They also will replace cash, checks, debit cards, and credit cards in paying for products and services of all kinds. Shoppers will simply point their WebPhone at the shop's portable reader to zap cash to its bank account.

The WebPhone – which my 1993 book *The Future Consumer* predicted as a "TeleCom Wallet" and which Bill Gates later proposed in 1996 as a "WalletPC" – will replace everything we now carry in our wallets and purses.

As mobile as your watch and as personal as your purse – but safer than either of them – your secure WebPhone will require either a fingerprint or a voice print to operate.

It will be worthless to a thief and, should it get lost, you'll have a ready backup copy at home.

The WebPhone thus will contain all your personal identification cards and papers such as driving licenses, social security/health information, and credit card data.

> **The WebPhone will not only transplant PCs as the dominant Web access tool.**
>
> **It will replace everything we now carry in our wallets and purses.**

As well, your WebPhone will store dozens of favorite family photos and will serve as your passport.

And, as an electronic wallet, the WebPhone essentially will put your bank account in your pocket.

As bank tellers and banking machines inevitably disappear – just like payphones – you'll download cash wirelessly to your WebPhone at any time no matter where you are. Cell phone users in Europe, Japan, and South Korea already do this.

In those countries, WebPhones also are used for shopping. Consumers use them to pay at vending machines, to buy coffee, pay for taxi rides – the list goes on.

All merchants – including Quixtar – will come to think of the mobile phone as a new retail outlet, right in their customers' pockets.

To shop online will be as simple as making a phone call – and almost all of us will do it.

The Future QUIXTAR Consumer

2

THE ECONOMIC WEBOLUTION
The Coming Home-Based Economy

COMMERCE AND COMMUNICATION are two sides of the same coin. And faster and better communication has always brought profound economic and business changes. The Webolution is dramatically changing the economic landscape and it will create abundant wealth for those who grasp it and position themselves to capitalize on it.

Beyond the Dot-Com "Bubble"

With the bursting of the dot-com stock market "bubble" in 2000-2001, many people became skeptical of the Internet's potential. So we need to understand what really happened, its impact on e-commerce (if any), and what comes next.

True, many people got caught up in the super-hype of a Web mania that became totally irrational. They drove stock prices to ridiculously overvalued levels. When the tech-laden NASDAQ index was rising towards 3000, I warned audiences that it already was way ahead of itself, too high, would inevitably correct, and that the higher it went the farther it would fall. It went to 5100 and then fell to 1100, wiping out many investor portfolios, companies, and jobs.

But much of the stock mania had little to do with dot-com start-ups and the Internet. Indeed, many Dow-listed stocks such as Coca Cola and Gillette traded at ridiculous prices and even solid tech stocks were driven sky high. Microsoft's CEO said publicly that his company's stock was overvalued; Amazon's CEO actually warned people not to buy his company's obviously overvalued stock. In short, the stock sell-off was long overdue, inevitable, salutary, and healthy.

In truth, the stock meltdown had three main elements. They are described fully in the latest edition of *Future Consumer.Com* and will not be repeated here.

Survival of the Fittest

In fact, the dot-com shakeout in the e-tailer sector was but one part of the "bubble." It weeded out the excesses and the weaklings. After all, how many online pet stores did we need? Yet, after reading some newspaper stories in 2000-

2001, you'd think the Internet had died. As we've seen since, the Webolution was far too big to go "poof" with the stock "bubble."

The untold story, again, is that – throughout 2001, 2002, 2003, and still today – consumers switch on brand new PCs, PDAs, and cell phones at the rate of three-per-second worldwide. Minute in, minute out, about 100 new people go online for the first time in their lives. AOL alone has at least one million people online at any minute of the day.

Every 7 seconds, a brand new online shopper buys something for the first time in their life. Minute in, minute out, e-shoppers are buying more than they've ever bought before.

Clearly, the 2000-2001 shakeout was only about 10 seconds after the Web's "big bang." It wrung the initial silliness out of the first phase of the new era but didn't slow down the Webolution one bit. The Web isn't even a toddler yet, never mind running, and it's going to live 100 years.

However, entry to e-commerce is becoming foreclosed because a few surviving Web pioneers dominate their sectors and have found out what works online.

Quixtar came out of the shakeout a big winner. Growing rapidly, and profitable from day one, it enjoys a big first-mover advantage.

> **Quixtar came out of the shakeout a big winner.**
>
> **Growing rapidly, and profitable from day one, it enjoys a big first-mover advantage.**

Web-Based Marketing and Distribution

The Web is absolutely perfect for a new buyer-centric, networked, mass-customized, one-to-one, relationship-based business model such as Quixtar.

By contrast, the old, factory-based, mass production, mass consumption, mass marketing, mass advertising economy is utterly obsolete. The Web blows it to bits.

The wireless Web transforms fixed assets such as buildings, machines, and telephone wires into "dead" capital with diminishing returns. And it turns online products and mobile human resources into "live" intellectual capital with increasing returns.

Only an online "high-touch + high-tech" networked business model such as Quixtar can fully exploit these new marketing and distribution dynamics.

The Web thus changes distribution channels by allowing customers to become "prosumers" who sell products to themselves and to each other.

Prosumer "Value Web"

That's because the Web boosts economic value to benefit both producer and consumer. Indeed, the online consumer becomes the producer – or what *The Third Wave* author Alvin Toffler long ago called the "prosumer" of value.

Quixtar is exactly the kind of prosumer-based business that is best suited to the Internet era.

Old, 2nd-wave, pre-Web product-driven companies boosted shareholder value by extracting it *from* customers.

The new, 3rd-wave post-Web, prosumer-driven company sees business owners and customers as complementary.

Prosumer businesses focus on lifetime customer value – which Web-enabled 1:1 marketing now permits. They see their customers as *assets* that generate ongoing streams of income.

> **Quixtar is exactly the kind of prosumer-based and prosumer-driven business that is best suited to the Internet era.**

In this way, prosumers drive growth in business value, and the Web provides a unique way of achieving that, as will be explained more fully in Chapter 7.

As well, the Web clearly and dramatically lowers the cost of business-to-consumer communication, reducing the cost of transactions and interactions between them.

In fact, the Web decouples the linear, industrial "value chain," reconfigures it into a "value web" and, in turn, restructures businesses into "value networks."

Quixtar's First-Mover Advantage

This phenomenon is something that Quixtar understood from the outset of online shopping, and it is harnessing the power of the Web to leverage business growth.

First movers in a networked industry – such as Quixtar – enjoy the "winner-take-all" benefit of exploiting "network effects" to achieve increasing returns. They carve out a competitive advantage by doing something that simply does not fit the old strategy framework.

Their competitive advantage stems from doing things differently from competitors in a way that delivers a unique type of value to customers – by offering different features, services, or logistical arrangements.

This is what the personalization, customization, home delivery, and one-to-one positioning elements of e-marketing strategies are all about – as perfectly demonstrated and executed by the likes of Quixtar.

The Web is simply destroying the old bases of competition. Traditional approaches to creating a sustainable competitive advantage will wither against this blistering pace of change.

The marketing mix also will change yet again to focus on a new value proposition: the time, convenience, personalization, and proximity of each individual prosumer in a networked economy. *(Again, these unique features are discussed at length in Chapter 7.)*

Winner-Take-All Websites

In parallel, consumers gravitate to a few favorite websites.

As some sites get busier (i.e., more popular), they simply attract more users. And the more users they attract, the richer and more useful they become – attracting yet more users in a virtuous cycle of digital capitalism where wealth begets more wealth.

The leading websites actually start to behave like a "brand." Sites such as Amazon, eBay, Quixtar, Yahoo and Google have in fact created new brand names which simply did not exist before. They've done it totally online, and often without any advertising.

The Web builds brands and amplifies wealth because it connects sellers and buyers more easily and on a scale never before possible.

This also produces a "winner-take-all" outcome where a few sites attract most business and the remainder get next to nothing. "Digital monopolies" seem inevitable because high-traffic websites will have few competitors. Hence, in any given business category, one or two players will come to dominate the market.

In many ways, then, the digital race is almost over before it begins. Once a strong leader is established in a category, outside of a big misstep it will build on its first-mover advantage to gain momentum and amass an insurmountable position.

Quixtar is a clear leader in all its product categories.

Consumers are voting with their mouse clicks for the Web economy and for Quixtar. About 70% of the North American economy involves personal consumption.

With nearly 5% of personal consumption already online, a brand-new $200 billion economic sector has been created.

The bigger the online shopping webolution becomes, it will transform the consumer economy in its wake, re-centering it back on the home.

Going Back to a Home-Based Economy

The pre-Industrial economy was almost entirely home-based. Before textile factories came along, families pooled their farm, spinning, and weaving profits to create a family income. They thus bound themselves together in common economic interest, strengthening the family structure.

But then newly-invented steam-powered machines came along. They required so much capital that the textile work became separated from home, centralized in factories.

For a while, the village economy operated much as before. Alone or in small teams, workers made customized products to the exact needs of an individual customer.

Even until the early 1800s, most consumer goods were still handmade within the family home.

But as transport networks improved, family self-sufficiency declined in favor of high street retailing. Between 1820 and 1850 there was an enormous growth in the number of shops, separating producer from consumer.

And the later growth of department stores also shifted retail business to large urban areas, to the detriment of local shopkeepers and markets.

Factories also led to the demise of home-made products: jam, pickles, cakes, bread, and dairy products, as well as clothing, draperies and simple furniture.

The Industrial Revolution thus changed where and how products were made, distributed, and consumed – and by whom.

The factory dramatically cut the cost of production, changing business models and creating rich industrialists.

The Webolution is reversing almost everything that the Industrial Revolution put in place.

It is re-centering the economy on the home.

The Web is a new opportunity where those who conduct commerce in novel ways will reap huge rewards.

> **The Web is a new opportunity where those who conduct commerce in novel ways will reap huge rewards.**

Web-Driven Super-Boom to 2020

As predicted in my 1989 book *G-Forces*, in 1993 the North American economy embarked on a Web-driven "Super-Boom" that will last until at least 2020.

This boom was interrupted or slowed down by 9/11 and the subsequent war on terrorism. But the boom will continue, probably with another slowdown around 2010, and then will run until around 2020 before it matures.

Indeed, the Webolution will have such a profound economic impact that wealth creation will be unprecedented during this period.

This wave of prosperity stems mainly from the productivity gains under Moore's Law and the network effect of the fast-growing Web – growth that will be magnified by more-efficient product marketing and distribution.

Indeed, every newly-connected online consumer increases the value of an e-shopping network to all its members. Collectively, they build their network at compound rates of growth.

Webpreneurs Weaving a Web of Wealth

A perfect example is the huge growth of the online auction house, eBay, which has created an e-cottage economy. As media guru Marshall McLuhan long ago observed:

> **"With computers, we are headed for cottage economics – where industrial activities can be carried on in any little shack, anywhere on the globe."**

The concept of cottage economics is entirely appropriate because, after all, the word "economy" derives from the Greek word for household.

Thanks to home-based webpreneurs, family life and economics is enjoying a renewal. Across North America, tens of millions of people have become determined to "get a life" – a "Web Life" – at home.

Every 11 seconds somebody starts a new home-based business in North America – that's 50,000 a week! Those who join them will ride the wave of the future.

Again, we can draw striking parallels with the textile revolution. Then, as in today's Web-driven economy, anyone with basic skills and a little money, and who was prepared to take a small risk, faced a bewildering array of opportunities to make money. Even the poorest family valued owning at least one handloom, the cost of which it could easily afford.

As looms became more complex, they were more expensive than earlier models and a loom bought this year could be obsolete the next.

Still, new looms produced more, and demand for output was so great that families owned several.

In time, the looms became cheaper and more efficient and families had one in every room of the house.

Every 11 seconds somebody starts a new home-based business – 50,000 a week!

Those who join them will ride the wave of the future.

Sound familiar?

Of course, new technology is a threat to those who lack it. And so it is with the PC and the Web.

Any family that doesn't own at least one PC is in danger of missing out on the biggest income bonanza in history.

That's because revolutionary technology – such as the Web – creates dramatic shifts in economic value, shifting producers and consumers in and out of the money stream.

Webpreneurs recognize that an online PC is a "golden loom" capable of weaving an ever-expanding web of e-business wealth for them and their families.

Incorporated Family Economic Units

The Web opens up a "desktop retailing" opportunity to anyone with a PC modem and a modicum of ambition.

> The Web opens up a "desktop retailing" opportunity to anyone with a PC modem and a modicum of ambition.

Clearly, home is where the future is.

And as commerce "comes back home," marriage and family will be much more of an economic endeavor, so much so that most families will legally incorporate as businesses.

Their pooled money will re-strengthen their families and lead to many fewer divorces.

An economically-focused "family values" movement is fast emerging. Families are changing their priorities to provide for day-care at home, home-based schooling and e-university education, to care for aging parents – and they want a financial base for their own retirement!

Families also are changing their shopping habits and starting home-based businesses which capitalize on the home shopping trend.

And these are not "mom and pop" shops. More and more families now see their home-based family business as a company – and feel good about owning it.

This quiet morphing of Web users into Webpreneurs is a major part of the Webolution.

After all, one billion people worldwide soon will be online. By 2010, that number will double to 2 billion, each potentially representing a family economic unit.

Consider, then, the possibility 2 billion family-owned prosumer businesses – comprising 4-5 billion lifelong e-shoppers – all potentially interacting through the Quixtar website for at least some of their everyday needs.

The mind boggles!

The Future QUIXTAR Consumer

3

THE SOCIAL WEBOLUTION
The Coming Web Lifestyle

B ILL GATES, CHAIRMAN OF MICROSOFT, predicted in mid-1997 that the majority of North Americans would be living a "Web Lifestyle" within 10 years – that is, by 2007 at the latest.

There is no reason to doubt Gates' prediction. After all, Microsoft is investing multi-billions of dollars a year in a "dot-Net" strategy to make this way of life possible. But can it all happen so quickly?

Gates himself says there is a tendency to *over*-estimate how much things will change in the short term (that's why we had the "bubble") but to *under*-estimate how much things will change over 10 years.

For sure, we're at a historic turning point, a true watershed in social and family affairs. The "Webolution" is an earth-shaking event that is dramatically reshaping our lives. We are living through the collapse of an outworn way of life and a new one being born.

Soon, all of us will be living our lives in even more fantastic ways.

The Internet is becoming the ubiquitous "dial tone" of everyday modern life, the rule rather than the exception.

Indeed, the Web extends personal space beyond the living room to the entire planet. Your computer is your world. And so the world is yours.

All of your interactions and transactions with everybody in the world, including those with your immediate family, will go through it. All your correspondence, billing records, product manuals, catalogs, family photographs and videos – everything, will be digitized.

Everyday Web Habit

Again, the "reversal" principle comes to bear. In the Internet age, you don't "go" to work. Work comes to you the moment you step into your home office and sit down with your always-on WebPC tablet, or WebPhone, or old-fashioned desktop PC.

Similarly, you don't "go" to school, the bank, the video rental store, or anywhere that you do not physically need to go. Thanks to the Web, they all come to you, electronically, no matter where you happen to be.

The Web opens up a global pathway for work, education, shopping, and recreation. The online family has a global database at its fingertips for children's homework, for cross-border online shopping, for tele-working across the globe, and for staying in constant touch with friends, relatives, and colleagues.

Just as we used to turn automatically to the radio, TV, or newspaper, most North Americans – yes *most* of us! – already use the Web daily, often several times a day, to check on weather, traffic, news, and sports.

A recent study showed that 90% of 5-17 year old kids in America are online!

Tens of millions of adults use the Web to manage their finances, watch their stocks, and file their tax returns. Even more millions use the Web to buy flowers, books, music, toys, clothing, and airline tickets – even cars.

In other words, 200+ million North Americans already use the Web in much the same way that others still use the postal service, the Yellow Pages, the telephone, or go to the bank and go shopping in stores.

Now, if someone asked you why you make phone calls, watch TV, drive a car, or go shopping, you'd think they were crazy. They are second nature; an integral part of life.

By 2007, the vast majority of us will take the Web for granted; we won't even notice it.

It will be second nature to turn to the Web for shopping, education, healthcare, entertainment, and to earn a living. Websites will be so sophisticated that interacting with them will be the most natural daily thing to do.

Computers will start to "disappear" in the sense that we now take automobiles, microwave ovens, toasters, and cell phones for granted.

Whenever we bring a new technology home – whether cell phone, answer machine, fax, or computer – it changes our ideas about convenience, about how we interact with the outside world, and about life itself.

Peek into your kid's room and you'll see the future. Like today's teens, we all will soon spend more time with our PCs than our TVs.

Many of us already do. We are becoming digitally-networked families.

The Digitally-Networked Family

The so-called nuclear family provided clear-cut, often rigid boundaries between private and public lives, between home and the outside world. The network family will be much different.

In the networked world, family must be seen as a network of people. As relatives disperse, the Web becomes the gathering place where extended families come together to celebrate births, catch up on relatives, organize weddings and re-unions, or mourn deaths.

Already, home pages and e-mails are used to share year-end letters and to show off baby photos and wedding albums.

The Web is sweeping aside TV as the family hearth. The Web is a digital hearth, and a different set of household rules and family practices is emerging.

For example, the social function of keeping up family contacts is gravitating online. Even members of the same household send e-mail messages to each other because they often aren't home at the same time.

In the future, families will be at home more often. But communication with extended family will go over

> **The extended e-family will unite through e-commerce and networked family business ventures.**

the Web. And the extended e-family will unite through e-commerce and networked family business ventures.

Families that Surf Together, Stay Together

The Webolution returns us to a family structure more like that of the Agricultural Age when life was home-based.

Children were educated at home, the sick were treated and cared for there, as were the elderly. Work took place in the home, not at some outside workplace.

The Industrial Revolution swiftly shifted work to the factory, and later to the factory-like office. Kids went to factory-like schools, the sick were put in factory-like hospitals and the elderly were "confined" in nursing homes.

The industrial-era family of breadwinner husband and home-maker/child-rearing wife will soon be a vestige of history. The edict of "job first, family second" only worked when the family depended on the breadwinner's single pay packet.

That work–family divide is rapidly being replaced by a new work–family compact where the Webolution makes the home again central to society.

Home-based commerce not only erases the separation of work and family; it also replaces workplace conformity with new family business roles and much more personal freedom.

People want a more-balanced life. Recent opinion polls show that only 58% of North Americans feel they have a satisfactory work–life balance. Indeed, 72% say they would work fewer hours if they could find a way to do so.

As a result – especially since 9/11 and the economic slowdown – there is a fast-growing urge by people to work at home, often for themselves.

For sure, the loyalty tie that once bound people to employers has snapped. People simply expect and demand greater personal autonomy. And they are sick and tired of commuting.

While the media still depict corporate career images to which some people still aspire, the Web lets people pursue their own family business and economic interests.

The Web Lifestyle allows people to develop interests and activities similar to those of family members, rather than those of work colleagues.

Families that are heavy Web users say they are more intact because they can work, play and learn together. **"Web Life" families grow together rather than apart.**

Additional specific benefits of a Web Lifestyle are several. For example, "work" and household chores such as shopping can be done on a much more flexible time schedule. And childcare is automatic within the home as opposed to sending the child out to a caregiver.

This flexibility lets families spend much more quality time together.

> **Families that are heavy Web users are more intact because they can work, play, learn together.**
>
> **"Web Life" families grow together rather than apart.**

In fact, Web Lifestyle families can't imagine life without the Web any more than they could imagine life without a cell phone or a car – or a digital home.

Digital Domiciles

Almost every home will be digitized. They will have "www" Internet domains that will be more important than street addresses, zip codes, and phone numbers.

Digital homes will have what computer people call a "server" – basically a PC that sits in a closet, utility room or basement, just like the electricity panel.

This server will connect – by wires or wirelessly – via a secure network to room outlets. It will monitor and control all multimedia traffic flowing in and out of the home to and from every appliance in the home. PCs and wireless portable devices, such as PC tablets and WebPhones, will communicate via the server.

Typical applications will include Web access, tele-commuting, distance learning, tele-medicine, video telephony, kitchen appliance management, security systems, power control, automated utility meter reading, lawn sprinklers, on-demand entertainment, online shopping, financial services and bill payment – the list goes on.

Flat-panel screen displays of various sizes scattered throughout the home will be your family's link to the outside world. You will shop online, watch movies, or say "Hi!" to Grandma, all by voice command.

And families will still "go shopping" together, except that they will do it virtually, from the comfort of their homes.

Online Fridges, "Talking" Shopping Carts ... and WebPhone Shopping Assistants

The family room and adjoining kitchen will continue to be the family communications hub. Walk into your kitchen and with a simple voice command you will scan your video messages from family and friends on a flat-panel display embedded in the countertop or in a cupboard or fridge door.

You'll know immediately where everyone is and when they will be home for dinner. The system will read out loud all your fax, e-mail, phone, and video doorbell messages. You will simply tell it which ones to save, print, or delete as you go along.

Your "smart" fridge – already on the market – will monitor its own contents and compile an electronic grocery list which, with a voice command, you can zap to your food delivery company.

The fridge also can let you know when it is running low on something like milk, sending you a voice-mail reminder to buy more on your way home.

If you still stubbornly insist on going to the supermarket or big box store, while there you will use your WebPhone to get a list from the fridge of all the groceries you need to buy as you browse the aisles. Your fridge has a tiny camera inside so you can see its contents on your WebPhone's display.

Personally, I don't think many of us will use all of these gadgets. And technology clearly can go too far. For example, **the next big horror coming to a supermarket near you is the "talking" shopping cart.** Invented in 2003 by IBM, and already on trial, it's likely to blurt out:

"Your favorite brand of spam is on sale in Aisle 6. Oh, and by the way, it's been 6 weeks since you bought any toilet paper!"

Millions of people are not waiting for these magical shopping assistants (or obnoxious shopping carts) to come along.

They are already online – click-happy shoppers, simplifying their lives, shopping at places like Quixtar.

The Future QUIXTAR Consumer

Part II

THE QUIXTAR SHOPPER

NOT ALL SHOPPERS ARE CREATED EQUAL. This part of the book has 2 chapters: one that explains the overall online shopping trend; and another that describes tomorrow's Quixtar consumer.

Some products and services are much easier to shop for online than others. But Quixtar is perfectly positioned to take advantage of some of the "hottest" segments of the online shopping product range.

At the same time, some types of shopper are more inclined than others to shop online.

The key to success in building a Quixtar business will be to understand prospective customers – and "what makes them click" online.

The Future QUIXTAR Consumer

4

THE ONLINE SHOPPING TREND
The "Ditto Delivery" Way

E VERY 7 SECONDS SOMEBODY NEW SHOPS ONLINE for the very first time in their life. Then they do it again and again.

As the "Webolution" rolls inexorably onward, on-line shopping is gathering strength. And, as we'll see later in Chapter 6, Quixtar is leading the way.

So, ask yourself, which would *you* rather do?

- **DRAG THE KIDS TO THE STORE**, shove a laden shopping cart with a wobbly wheel up and down crowded aisles, wait in line at the checkout (prompting a toddler meltdown), then hump all the stuff home – some 3 hours later;

... or, would you rather ...

- **DRAG THE STUFF INTO AN ONLINE SHOPPING CART** with your mouse, faster than writing up a shopping list, then kick back with the kids until it arrives on your doorstep – at the time you select.

It's a no-brainer, right?

The Web is fast becoming a shopper's paradise, changing not only how people buy, but how often, when, what, why, and from where.

By 2010, the majority of us will do much of our shopping online. And, as forecast in *Future Consumer.Com*, the Web will gobble nearly 30% of retail sales by then.

Indeed, those who become Quixtar "prosumers" will buy most things from their very own online store!

Surge in Online Shopping

Until the Industrial Revolution, there were few shops of any kind. Most people grew their own crops, raised their own chickens, cured their own bacon, milked their own cows, baked their own bread and cookies, made their own jam and preserves, even tailored, sewed, and knit their own clothing.

They were "prosumers" who consumed their own produce.

As mentioned earlier, the factory-based economy changed all that, bringing high street shops and then malls.

The Web is changing it all again. And 9/11 reinforced the change, driving about 11 percent of shoppers to do *all* of their 2001 holiday shopping online from home rather than risk going out to malls. And that trend has continued.

More than 60% of North American Internet users – that's 130 million people! – have bought a product online, up from 49% at the end of 2000. As well, 80% of online shoppers say they save oodles of time by shopping online.

While habits don't change easy, people gradually are altering their shopping routine. And as more families come to appreciate the time, convenience, and safety of e-shopping, online sales will only grow.

For sure, whether e-shopping is "for real" is over. While estimates vary, $62 billion was spent online in 2001, double that of 2000. That rose to $94 billion in 2002 and to $128 billion in 2003.

While still small relative to total retail sales, online shopping could reach $200 billion by 2005 and will kick in big time after then, growing fast to top $1 trillion by 2010.

By 2010, online sales will be 300 times bigger than in 2000 – a tidal wave of e-commerce that will make megabucks for online winners.

e-Shopping at the Online Winners

The rewards of e-commerce will accrue fastest to those who embrace it first. For sure, "first-movers" such as

Quixtar have left their online *and* offline competitors in catch-up mode.

> **Quixtar is one of the few that not only survived the dot-com crucible but went from strength to strength as more and more people were attracted to it.**

When everything collapses, you need to look around and see what's left standing. See who not only survived but who is still prospering.

And among the dot-com companies, Quixtar is one of the few that not only survived the dot-com crucible but went from strength to strength as more and more people were attracted to it.

Shoppers are gravitating in growing numbers to online successes such as Quixtar – building them into winners. And they are spending more online than they have spent before.

Web Shopping Goes Mainstream

The Web has become an accepted purchase medium and people are not going to stop shopping online any more than they will stop using the Web, toss out their PCs and cell phones, or stop driving their cars.

Online shopping is becoming part of everyday life. It is going mainstream.

The Internet takes shopping out of the shops. In turn, of course, that takes the shops out of shopping and brings them right into your home.

Your Web-connected PC becomes your shop – a virtual showroom for comparison-shopping and convenient buying. And it is stocked with everything from vintage wine to brand new cars.

By comparison, in-store shopping is a pain: crowded parking lots and store aisles, freezing-cold or steamy-hot weather, tired feet, endless check-out lines, "out of stock" products, and disinterested, discourteous, clueless store clerks – not to mention the drain on your time.

The incentive to escape all that frustration and go online is very strong, regardless of what you're shopping for. You can search for and buy goods from a host of world-wide merchants through your PC at any time of day or night. Web shops like Quixtar never close.

Products Most Suitable for Online Sale

Beyond what we know about what's already selling online, basic common sense tells us what kinds of products are a "no-brainer" to buy online. Some items obviously may be more suitably bought online than others, depending on three related factors, listed below:

1. HOW COMPLEX is the product or service to research, understand, and purchase?

The Web is an info-intensive, highly efficient, multi-medium – a perfect channel for at least researching, if not buying, almost any product or service.

2. HOW EASY OR INEXPENSIVE is the product to ship to your home – or for you to return if you don't want it?

Products other than purely digitized ones – such as software, music, books, or videos – still must be physically delivered to the home.

But even if you needed a bucket of nails, on which the shipping costs would be prohibitive, you could still order online and then pick them up at the store, maybe at a drive-through. And, as now, you can always return any product you don't want.

3. DO YOU REALLY NEED to see, touch, try on, or test the product?

That can be true for fresh grocery items, some clothing, furniture, appliances, and major purchases such as cars and homes.

But not everybody needs to squeeze tomatoes, try on new slacks, lie down on a new bed, test drive a car, or walk through a home before buying it.

Today, all these products are being bought online, sight unseen.

Four Product Types

Products also fall into four groups: convenience, replenishment, researched, and subjective items.

Let's briefly review each in turn, with special emphasis on replenishment items – Quixtar's forté.

1. CONVENIENCE ITEMS

Light-weight, don't-need-to-research, convenience items are the easiest to buy online and to deliver to your home. Examples of hot-selling convenience items include books, music, videos, airline and event tickets, toys, flowers, and gifts. **About 90% of Web surfers have bought books online and, in 2003, 16% of the dollar value of books was bought on the Web, as were 10%-12% of travel and event tickets.**

2. REPLENISHMENT ITEMS

The next easiest products to buy online are replenishment items – non-perishable food, cleaning products, health and beauty items, etc.

Almost all the items in this category are on Quixtar's product list.

Best of all, replenishment items require no research once the first purchase has been made. Happy with the product, you buy it again and again, almost without thinking about it.

Just think about how many of the items in your supermarket shopping cart are the very same items you buy over and over again, week in, week out. Why not just have them delivered?

Sure, a few replenishment items are a tad heavy and might incur above-average shipping costs.

But *most* replenishment items are lightweight and so an overall order is in fact inexpensive to ship on a cost-per-item basis.

3. RESEARCHED ITEMS

Slightly more difficult to buy online are items such as insurance, mortgages, or computer hardware and software. They are easy to deliver, either digitally online or by courier. But they tend to be complex and require some thought. Still, the Web is very effective in helping you with that research, and many of these items are bought online. **In 2003, for example, more than 50% of stock trades were done online and 32% of computer hardware and software was bought online.**

4. SUBJECTIVE ITEMS

The most difficult items to buy online and have delivered to the home tend to be bulky, heavy products. They also tend to be more expensive. Examples are furniture, appliances, and cars. But even these items are bought online, sight unseen.

Clearly, then, every product type is already being bought online. One reason is that the Web lets you interact with the product.

For example, Amazon lets you peek inside books and to submit personal preferences of book genres or authors to get automatic notification of new books or suggested titles of interest.

The Web also helps you buy products that are more personalized or customized to your tastes and needs. Dell lets you custom-build your PC online and the car makers are planning to let you do the same.

You can also interact with companies online and get personalized assessments of your needs. For example, Quixtar's "Ask the Expert" feature links to Johns Hopkins University where you select the right nutritional product for your needs. You can also fill out "personal assessments" of your eating habits, stress factors, and overall lifestyle. Quixtar then analyzes this information and sends you a personalized portfolio of suggested products.

There really is no excuse not to shop online. Soon, most of us will be shopping this way, not just for books, PCs, and nutritional products, but for most everyday needs, including groceries and beauty items.

Health & Beauty Needs

To see why everyday products are so suitable for online shopping, let's just review this one example.

Health and beauty supplies are natural to buy online because they're info-intensive, mostly nonperishable, easy and cheap to ship, and need frequent replacement.

Indeed, in dollar terms, healthcare is a larger online business than books and music, and e-pharmacies carry huge selections of everything from aspirin to cosmetics to vitamins.

The overall healthcare market was about $640 billion in 2003, including neutraceuticals, vitamins, and health and beauty aids. This will reach at least $1 trillion by 2007, and most of that will be sold online.

Direct sellers and network marketers such as Quixtar are positioned to become the dominant distributors of wellness and nutritional products that health-conscious and weight-conscious people are now using in record numbers.

> **Direct sellers and network marketers such as Quixtar are positioned to be the dominant distributors of wellness and nutrition products.**

The cosmetics segment also is booming online. Online drugstores quite naturally are adding beauty sections to their product line-up in an attempt to capture some of the $13 billion that North Americans spent on cosmetics in 2003.

Many in the industry debate whether women will swap the personal attention they get at cosmetics counters for the click of a mouse.

Again, as indeed in all Web-threatened sectors, dismissive claims that "you can't smell anything over the Internet" or that "colors don't look so good on a screen" don't stand scrutiny.

True, the cosmetics industry has traditionally relied heavily on the "touchy-feely" aspects of its products. Free samples are liberally distributed at cosmetics counters and customers often try the product to get a feel for the colors and textures of each brand.

But 70% of cosmetic sales are repeat business: once the customer knows what she likes, she simply buys refills.

Generally speaking, cosmetics shoppers also buy names that they have come to like, and most consumers know exactly what the products are.

Moreover, particularly for commodity items such as lipstick and nail polish, most people find one brand and keep on using it. **For such products, the Internet is a perfectly natural and ideal sales channel.**

The online beauty boom mainly will be driven by women – particularly young women – who are flocking to the Internet and now outnumber men both as surfers and online shoppers.

Cosmetics sites particularly appeal to a younger, tech-savvy consumer who is pressed for time. She is more likely to shop if she doesn't have to leave her home or office, particularly when she is merely replacing products that otherwise would be a hassle to buy.

Quixtar is not without competition from the likes of Avon, Mary Kay, and Herbalife in this category.

But it has a vast and established client base for vitamins, cosmetics, and other health and beauty items in this category and it undoubtedly will be a top online supplier.

– • –

Now that we have a clearer understanding of what people buy online, and why, let's explore who is shopping online – and what makes them "click."

The Future QUIXTAR Consumer

5

THE FUTURE
QUIXTAR CONSUMER
On the e-Shopping "Learning Curve"

QUIXTAR SHOPPERS ARE ABOVE AVERAGE and well ahead on the e-shopping "learning curve."

No, I am not privy to data on Quixtar shopper profiles, which the company keeps confidential. But the research used for this chapter probably is at least generally typical of Quixtar shoppers. And certainly, in terms of purchasing power and online shopping enthusiasm, anecdotal evidence and website audience research show that Quixtar shoppers are indeed above average.

So let's see how the demographic, psychographic, and webographic shopper profiles help us understand who will be the best Quixtar shopping prospects.

Five Consumer Generations

Each generation of people bears a strong imprint of the era in which it is born and raised – and tends to assume, quite wrongly, that its life experience is the norm for everyone.

In fact, society changes with the mood of the times, and economic circumstances shape attitudes about how parents raise the next generation.

Technology also conditions consumer behavior and shapes expectations.

While no generation has precise boundaries, in North America there are 5 fairly clear birth cycles.

1. "BY-the-BOOK" *(born 1911–1928)*

Most of these folks, too set in their ways to change, distrust the Web. Few of them go online for any purpose.

Most of this group is *unlikely* to shop online.

2. "BY-the-CLOCK" *(born 1929–1945)*

Half of this clock-driven group used a PC during their work years and many have Web access at home for e-mail. They also surf for weather, healthcare and investment information. Half of them buy books and software online, and some even buy cars online. The younger members of the group clearly enjoy online shopping's convenience. But most of the oldsters won't go online until access is easier and, even then, will only buy simple stuff, such as toys for grandkids.

The *younger* members of this group are more like Baby Boomers in going online to shop and, hence, are good Quixtar prospects.

3. "BABY-BOOM" *(born 1946–1964)*

Feeling and acting at least 10 years younger than did their parents at the same age, Boomers are active online. Their values were heavily influenced by TV in their youth, but they became PC literate in the workplace. At home they've embraced PCs and cell phones and gravitated naturally online. Always ready to shift to the latest trend, they are ditching old media in favor of the empowering Web. They live active lifestyles and, upon entering middle age, are much concerned with health and finances. Being skeptical of mass marketing claims and conflicting "expert" views, they go online to learn for themselves the reality behind product claims. They then tend to buy online as well.

With money to spend, Boomers are excellent Quixtar shopping prospects. And those with higher education and management/supervisory or marketing/sales experience are strong IBO business-builder candidates.

4. "GEN-X" *(born 1965–1982)*

A typically counterculture generation, Gen-X grew up fast as "latch-key" kids and the children of divorce. They learned to fend for themselves and are self-sufficient in almost every way. While they used to hang out in shopping malls during their teens, many now reject "mallism." Escaping the "traditional," Gen-X people love PCs and online shopping, especially as they start their own families.

Gen-X is entrepreneurial and will not only shop online but gravitate naturally to building a strong Quixtar business.

5. "WEB-GEN" or "GEN-Y" (born 1983–2001)

These young people automatically represent tomorrow's online shoppers. Never having known a world without PCs, cell phones, and the Web, this "digital generation" surfs almost by instinct. They are the quintessential "future consumer.com." As the group ages – about five million new car drivers will come of age annually until 2010 – marketers of every product will have to come to grips with quite different consumer expectations. Endlessly searching for and adopting new ideas, they are the most likely to use the Web and any new e-gadget that comes along.

For Web-Gen, online shopping is the *only* way to shop. They'll be avid Quixtar shoppers and gung-ho IBOs.

e-Shopping is Going Mainstream

Apart from the most elderly, then, almost everybody's going online and shopping. The profile of North America's 200+ million Internet users now pretty much mirrors society at large – as do the 130 million online shoppers.

Of the online population at the end of 2003, by age group, the following had shopped online at least once:

- **43%** of 16–22 year-olds
- **57%** of 23–29 year-olds
- **66%** of 30–44 year-olds
- **52%** of 45–59 year-olds
- **16%** of 60+ year-olds.

In sum, apart from the oldest seniors, e-shopping is now a main-stream activity.

As this trend continues, families with kids become a much more important market. About 40% of North American households have children, and about 62% of online households with kids are already shopping online.

These families have above-average income and higher levels of education.

They are a tech-savvy segment with strong purchasing power.

Until about 2002, their favorite online purchase categories were toys, event tickets, sports equipment, and music.

But these families have since moved to more mainline family products.

> **Online families with kids become a much more important market.**
>
> **62% of such households are already shopping online.**

As e-shopping continues to surge in parallel with the aging of this tech-savvy generation, the addition of their kids as teenage consumers in their own right, over the next decade, will greatly expand the sales volume of most if not all online product categories.

Quixtar, in appealing to this younger demographic group, is well positioned to take advantage of the growth.

Women and Minority Groups

Perhaps more significant, in the economy at large, women either make or influence 80% of all household purchases – equivalent to $2.7 trillion annually.

There are now more women online than men – 64% at the end of 2003, versus only 5% in 1994. As well, women did 69% of online shopping in full-year 2003, with this rising to 82% over the year-end holiday season.

Hence, women will utterly dominate online shopping. And they by far represent the best e-marketing opportunity for Quixtar.

Moreover, women have the spending power: more than 75% of women deal with household financial matters. Women increasingly are becoming homeowners in their own right and are greatly involved in all aspects of managing the household, including home improvement projects and their financing.

> **Women will utterly dominate online shopping.**
>
> **And they by far represent the best e-marketing opportunity for Quixtar.**

As well, the average female surfer earns nearly $60,000 a year. Indeed, the U.S. Bureau of Labor Statistics reports that 27% of women bring home a bigger paycheck than their husband, up from 17% in 1990, and half of them earn 50+% of their household's income.

With such purchasing power, the growth in women e-shoppers signals a major spur to online shopping.

As well, people of African, Asian, Hispanic/Latino, and Middle Eastern descent are now going online at a faster pace than the overall population.

Already, about 46% of African-American and Hispanic households are online. But even their online presence is dwarfed by the 84% of tech-savvy Asian-American households already on the Web – most of them also active e-shoppers.

"Super-Cool" Multimedium

Rapid technical advances are making all North American consumers more sophisticated and knowledgeable buyers.

Any consumer born since World War II has grown up in an increasingly visually-intensive, interactive multimedia world. As the "Web World" unfolds, prevalent old-fashioned marketing concepts simply won't work.

Desensitized to mass media message bombardment, consumers armed with online information not only reject but ridicule most advertising, dismissing it as hype and rejecting its blatant overstatement and hypocrisy.

It's often said that consumers spend more when they "sell products to themselves." The Web equips consumers to do exactly that. Moreover, Quixtar shoppers literally do sell products to themselves. They buy them from their own e-business.

Hence, mass advertising, promotional hype and aggressive sales are turned on their head by the Web. Any business that fails to understand this is doomed.

The Web is a "cool" medium that will become even "cooler." E-marketers must understand what "super-cool" Web shopping and personal distribution and relationship selling are all about.

And Quixtar's word-of-mouth, word-of-modem, 1:1 model is ideally suited to this new super-cool environment.

The Online Shopping "Learning Curve"

It still takes time for people to go online and start shopping. But once they do start buying online, there's no stopping them.

In the beginning, however, people gingerly go online and start finding their way around. It's just like when people move into a new neighborhood; they have to get to know the local stores and where to find things.

Usually thanks to a friend's e-mail suggestion, their first online purchase will be a book from Amazon. Most first-time buyers go to Amazon because a book is an easy thing to buy sight unseen, and because Amazon has a high reputation for security and privacy protection.

Once they've learned how to register with the site and fill out the order form, they click through the book order and then wait about a month before they buy anything else. They wait for the book to arrive and then for their credit card statement showing that they were billed correctly and that nobody else has used their credit card number.

Surfers thus gradually gain confidence and feel secure about giving out personal information. Feeling more secure, the new online shoppers then venture out to buy something else, either from Amazon, or eBay, or one of the other better-known websites. As they build confidence and gain experience, they become frequent online shoppers.

The Online "Learning Curve"

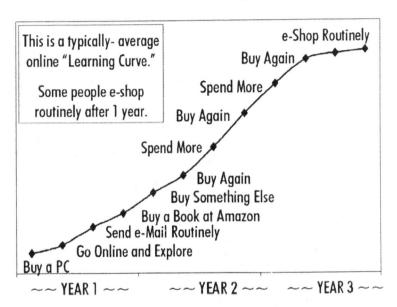

> This is a typically- average online "Learning Curve."
>
> Some people e-shop routinely after 1 year.

e-Shop Routinely
Buy Again
Spend More
Buy Again
Spend More
Buy Again
Buy Something Else
Buy a Book at Amazon
Send e-Mail Routinely
Go Online and Explore
Buy a PC

~~ YEAR 1 ~~   ~~ YEAR 2 ~~   ~~ YEAR 3 ~~

More They Buy ... the More They Buy

A consumer's preference for online shopping clearly improves substantially after their first purchase. In fact, research shows that they are *at least five times more likely* to buy again online than they were *before* their first purchase.

The first e-shoppers were the first Web users – the so-called "early adopters" – who were tech-savvy, intelligent, and curious people who are always the first to try something new. Besides their optimism, these consumers always want what's new and different, unique, innovative or surprising; they look for "cool" websites and products.

These smart e-shoppers also tended to be the better-educated consumers with higher-than-average incomes.

Although this group is now outnumbered by many latecomers such as women, it is still the out-front group on the online shopping "learning curve." They simply have been online the longest and are very accomplished e-shoppers who tend to buy many things online, including big ticket items.

For all online shoppers, however, the frequency with which they shop online and the amount of money they spend are both increasing rapidly.

Hence, the available market of online consumers for a whole variety of products is constantly expanding, as is the pool of money being spent. And as the first-time buyer often is introduced to online shopping by another more-experienced online shopper, so the network effect builds out the retail e-commerce economy.

By their nature, networkers are articulate folks, plugged into a web of sources for word-of-modem product recommendations. They make ideal customers for a network marketing opportunity such as Quixtar.

Converting Browsers to Buyers

As people become more experienced in the online world, the amount of time they spend online increases. For example, those who have been online more than 3 years spend about 20+ hours a week online compared to less than 5 hours for newcomers. And online shoppers have about 11 months more online experience than non-shoppers.

Converting browsers to buyers clearly takes time. Households that have been online less than 6 months comprise about 15% of the online population but account for only 3% of online purchases. Conversely, households that have been online for at least 2 years comprise 48% of the online population and account for more than 70% of online purchases.

As well, many of us buy products *offline* after researching them *online*. For every purchase made online, two additional purchases are researched.

Of course, as in the brick-n-mortar world, some researched items never get bought at all, either online or offline.

However, in-store shoppers are gradually shifting to online shopping.

> **The frequency with which people shop online and the amount of money they spend are both increasing rapidly.**

In 1996, for example, for every 10 people who "browsed and bought online," another 16 people "browsed online but bought *offline*." But this 10:16 ratio has dropped annually, falling to 10:9 in 2000 and to 10:3 in 2003.

This consistent trend shows that consumers are gaining great confidence in online shopping.

How Much Will People Spend Online?

Online sales are growing by 20%-30% per year, which is 10+ times faster than retail sales at large.

As recent as 2001, online sales accounted for only 2.5% of total retail sales. But due to their much more-rapid rate of growth, online sales as a percentage of total retail sales reached 3.4% in 2002 and rose again to 4.5% in 2003 *(see chart opposite)*.

The trend is clearly up, but where will this number go from here?

Many forecasts say online sales will account for, say, only 8% of total retail sales by 2007, or 10% by 2010. Such forecasts ignore and/or underestimate the ongoing effects of the social, technical and economic "webolutions" (detailed in Part I of this book) and are far too conservative.

The food and beverage category alone is expected to take off rapidly during the next 5 years, growing from about $5 billion in 2003 to $20+ billion by 2008.

As well, many online sales statistics and forecasts exclude several hot-selling and high-priced items, such as airline tickets, hotel bookings, and online sales of cars.

For example, online retail sales data published by the U.S. Department of Commerce exclude these items, as do data from some private sector agencies, thus badly underestimating online sale volume.

A more reasonable forecast comes from Martha Rogers, co-author of *One to One Marketing*, who believes that consumer-direct marketing will account for 24% of retail sales by 2010.

In the 2002 edition of *Future Consumer.Com*, I predicted that 29.5% of total retail sales, on a product category-weighted basis, will occur online by 2010.

I am sticking with that forecast for now.

The chart shows my current forecast of online sales for 2004-2010 as a percentage of total retail sales. My sales data include everything bought online by consumers.

Online Sales as % of Total Retail Sales

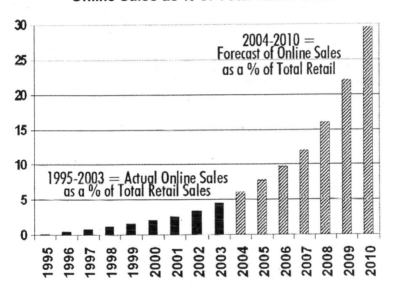

To give this forecast a "reality check," we can expect 90% of North American households to shop online by 2010 for at least something, and that 70% will be active shoppers.

On average, if just those active households each spend a modest $280 a week online by then – forget everybody else – that alone tallies to $1.2 trillion.

By 2010, total retail sales will be about $4.0 trillion. And $1.2 trillion is 30% of $4.0 trillion.

So I think my 29.5% forecast is realistic, based on current trends.

Even if I am only half right, 15% sold online would be a massive ongoing economic shift – three times as much sold online as in 2003.

Even if only 10% of total retail sales are sold online by 2010, that's twice as much as today – and still a fantastic e-commerce opportunity for businesses such as Quixtar.

Wouldn't you like to at least double or triple your Quixtar business by 2010? How about making your business six times as big as today?

Based on present trends, the opportunity is there for the taking.

Part III

THE QUIXTAR BUSINESS
The "Future Perfect" Opportunity

AFFILIATE MARKETING WITH QUIXTAR is what I call a "future perfect" opportunity for most people who want to own their own business. That's because, as demonstrated in this book, it is perfectly in sync with the "webolutionary" trends at play.

Part III describes Quixtar's spectacular and ongoing success story and then explores the options open to those wanting to build their own Quixtar business.

Please take your time in reading Part III. It is the most important part of the book. But if you've skipped the earlier chapters, you will not place Quixtar in the proper "big picture" context. So please take time to read the earlier material.

The Future QUIXTAR Consumer

6

THE QUIXTAR
SUCCESS STORY

Q UIXTAR IS A SPECTACULAR online shopping
and business success story, no matter how you
measure it. Look at total sales *(incl. Partner Stores)*:

- **2000** *(first online year)*: **Fast-track to $518 million** (versus Amazon's $147 million and eBay's $32 million in sales in *their* first year!).
- **2001: Leaped to $816 million** – remarkable amid a dot-com shakeout, a stock market meltdown, an economic slowdown, and 9/11.
- **2002: Climbed to $958 million.**
- **2003: Soared past the billion mark, to $1.1 billion.**

In only its first 4 years, Quixtar thus racked up $3.4
billion in total sales – and was profitable from day one!

The Quixtar Sales Track Record

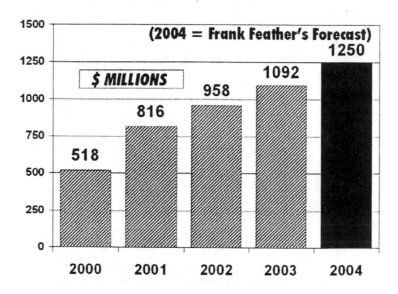

The 6 Main Keys to Quixtar's Success

What are some of the secrets of this astonishing perform-ance? Quixtar's success is based on six main factors:

1. **Product Range:** Non-perishable, replenishment, consumable items, all ideally suited to online shopping;

2. **"Ditto Delivery":** Regular, standing-order, direct shipment of product to the customer's doorstep;

3. **Value Package:** Reasonably-priced items on which the buyer earns a commission or bonus, plus a further bonus on referred sales.

4. **Effective Website:** A functional, fun, easy-to-use website that can be personalized.

5. **Tech-Savvy Positioning:** Attracting younger, multi-ethnic, tech-savvy, IBOs suitable for mentoring and personal development via a knowledge-rich "high-tech/high-touch" training program.

6. **One-to-One Networking:** Based on "high-touch" personal relationships of IBOs and customers.

As we'll see in the next chapter, these 6 factors perfectly mirror what I call the "6 Ps of e-Marketing" in general. But first let's explore each of them, specific to Quixtar itself.

Ideal e-Shopping Product Range

Quixtar offers a wide selection of reasonably priced, non-perishable, replacement-item consumables that are perfect for the online retail world.

Examples are cleaning products, skin care and cosmetics items, and vitamins and wellness products – just the kinds of things people buy repeatedly and which are easy to ship to the customer.

No list of products can do justice to everything that Quixtar has available, which is virtually anything a family might ever need. To begin with, the website offers Quixtar's own exclusive brands in 4 main sections:

- **Home:** A whole range of laundry, furniture, floor, kitchen, bathroom, auto, and multi-purpose cleaners and polishes, with SA8 laundry products being the best-known Quixtar brand in this group.

- **Health:** The well-known Nutrilite multivitamins, minerals, and herbal supplements, as well as weight management and performance foods.

- **Self:** Artistry range of cosmetic/skin care products and Satinique hair care items, plus designer fragrances, bath and body lotions, soap and toothpaste – plus Personal Accents jewelry.

- **Options:** Drugstore-type items such as over-the-counter remedies, feminine and infant care items, paper products, storage wraps/bags, pet food, batteries, and even hosiery – the list is endless.

That's only the start. In **"Store for More"** you can rethink your fashion wardrobe, revitalize your living space with bedding, furniture, and appliances, shop for lawn and garden supplies, vacuums, fitness equipment, and more.

You also can find great buys at Quixtar's **"Partner Stores"** – about 100 of them. Better-known names include DisneyStore.com, Office Max, KBtoys, Hickory Farms, IBM, Franklin Mint, Craftsman Tools, MCI, Sony Music, and Whirlpool. **Quixtar is your way to shop online at these brand-name stores!**

Last but not least, Quixtar offers products and services for businesspeople through a B2B or **"Business to Business"** solutions section.

No wonder Quixtar's sales are growing so strongly. And any and all of the above products are available for doorstep delivery.

"Ditto Delivery" to the Doorstep

As discussed earlier, and as the above lists show, most of the items we buy are convenience or replenishment items that we buy over and over again, week in, week out.

We write out the same shopping list every week and trudge off to spend two hours in a supermarket, gathering up hefty items, almost walking the aisles blindfolded to pick them off the same shelf as last week.

Supermarkets, of course, are a fairly recent invention – as are packaged goods. Previously, most products came from a general store, grocer or butcher. They were weighed out, item-by-item, order-by-order, by the shopkeeper who often delivered the orders to customers' homes.

In *Future Consumer.com* I recounted how my mother did the family shopping in 1950s England. I'll only briefly summarize it here.

She had two small Order Books. Each week, she wrote out her order list on a fresh page in one of the books: 1-lb sugar, 1-lb butter, 2-lb flour, etc. The grocer weighed out each product into plain brown bags and put them into a wooden crate for delivery to the house.

My mother paid the delivery boy for the amount tallied in the *first* Order Book and handed him the *second* Order Book that listed *next* week's items. And so it went: take delivery of one week's order; send back next week's.

But, as you can see from her lists *(overleaf)* her orders never varied much from one week to the next. She ordered much the same items as before. In fact, 90% of the items on each page in both books were the same, week in, week out.

I once asked her why she just didn't send the same list back again, rather than copying it out each time. Or just give the shopkeeper a "standing order" for items she just needed replenishing.

She said that would be handy, but the lists, with the grocer's prices entered alongside each product, helped her remember what to buy and to manage her budget. She also could vary the items and their quantities however she liked.

My Mother's Weekly Shopping Order Books
("Ditto Delivery" – circa 1950)

Order Book #1

JAS HEATON & SONS			
Greengrocers			
Customer Name		Date	
MRS. S. D. FEATHER		APRIL 7 1950	
√ Item	Amount	Price Per	Total £ - s - d
√ Sugar	1 LB	1s	1 - 0
√ Butter	½ LB	2s	1 - 0
√ Flour	2 LB	6d	1 - 0
√ W Bean			

Order Book #2

JAS HEATON & SONS			
Greengrocers			
Customer Name		Date	
MRS. S. D. FEATHER		APRIL 14 1950	
√ Item	Amount	Price Per	Total £ - s - d
√ Sugar	2 LB	1s	2 - 0
√ Butter	½ LB	2s	1 - 0
√ Flour	1½ LB	6d	9
√ W Bean		6d	

The Webolution returns us exactly to those days!

You now can order not just replenishment items but any product online by simply checking off boxes on an automatic re-order list and then have it all delivered.

It's far quicker than writing up a brand new list, for a needless trip to the supermarket, and you can better manage your household budget.

Supermarkets fail to grasp the customer demand for this kind of service. Only one in four supermarkets offers any kind of home shopping or home delivery program. Yet most people consider grocery shopping a chore. Out of 22 household tasks, one study found that grocery shopping came in next to last, just ahead of house cleaning. Shoppers simply don't enjoy grocery shopping.

By contrast, about 30% of online consumers have already bought at least some grocery products online. For them, two hours a week of supermarket hell have been transformed into a click-happy ten minutes online.

Supermarkets are a huge waste of time and most consumers want to win back that time to spend it with their families. And Quixtar's "Ditto Delivery" system allows them to do just that.

How Quixtar's "Ditto Delivery" Works

"Ditto Delivery" is a system designed for online shoppers and for Quixtar IBO business builders. To that end, it follows a simple process which, once you get it set up, operates virtually automatically.

The system first lets you analyze your household needs – a one-time process, as shown here.

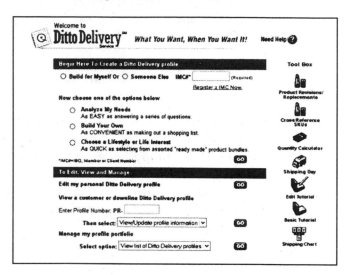

Then you compile a standing order "Ditto Delivery" list, which you can vary at any time later to suit your product or budget needs, as shown in this partial sample.

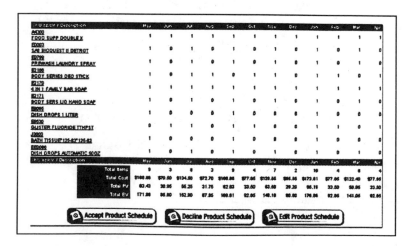

Now, if you are an IBO, you will want to track the Point Value (PV) on the purchases you make, and also of those made by others that you register into your business.

The system does that automatically for you, and forecasts it out into the future, as shown here.

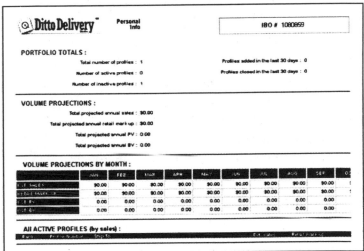

This ability to forecast PV is essential to driving and managing the growth of your business, as will be discussed in Chapter 7.

Such automatic replenishment or "ditto delivery" of grocery products will have a profound effect on their distribution and marketing.

It's inevitable that online grocery shopping will take off. As mentioned earlier, the food and beverage category alone is expected to take off rapidly during the next 5 years, growing from $5 billion in 2003 to $20+ billion by 2008.

And Quixtar is positioned to grab the market, especially in non-perishable goods.

What About Quixtar's Prices?

Product pricing needs to be seen in proper context.

Many consumers have been brainwashed (by constant "Sale" signs and "lowest" price claims) to seek out bargains. They do so on the mistaken assumption they are *saving* money, when in reality they are *over-spending*!

They also tend to think – even though they've never checked it out – that some online product prices are high.

Believe me: "big box" stores are profit-driven. Their so-called discount or "lowest" prices are to lure you down aisles stacked with enticing but high-margin items, on which the store makes most of its profit. Consumers get seduced into impulsive purchases – "into the bargain," so to speak! – and end up with closets full of useless stuff.

Consumers also totally overlook the hidden costs of shopping: gas for the car, wear and tear on the vehicle, and on your footwear – and probably a coffee and snack. Such hidden expenses easily outweigh the delivery charge on a "Ditto Delivery" order.

True comparison shopping – based on total value, not simplistic price – should recognize *all* product facets: quality, utility, money-back guarantees, the convenience of home delivery, cost "per unit" or "per use," etc.

Make fair allowance for demonstrable differences and you find that *any* product – if it is to succeed in the market over time – simply *has* to be competitive, no matter who sells it. And so it is with most Quixtar products.

Sure, online shopping companies like Quixtar also are in business to make money. So are their IBOs!

Value Package of IBO Commission

Quixtar rewards IBOs with a commission or bonus plus incentives (totaling about 28% of sales) on goods bought by and through them, based on product Point Value (PV). The more people you help get started as IBOs, the more sales you generate together and the greater your income.

IBOs thus prosper by changing their shopping habits – buying what they've bought all along, except now from their own Quixtar business rather than from elsewhere – and by getting others to do likewise.

And look at these rewards!

Dramatic Growth in Payouts to IBOs

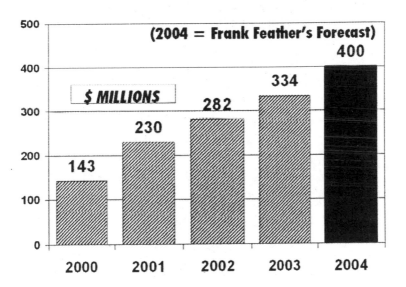

Total up those bars! In only 4 years, Quixtar has paid out $989 million in bonuses and incentives. A billion bucks and counting! Do you want a piece of that action?

Quixtar's "I-Commerce" Model

An IBO thus earns streams of income through what Quixtar calls its **"I-Commerce" model**, which converges these four key elements:

- **Internet**
- **Individual**
- **Infrastructure** (product distribution and support)
- **Independent Business Ownership** (IBOs)

This model lets webpreneurs own a turnkey Web-based business, without the expense of a website of their own, or any product development or distribution headaches.

Quixtar's e-business model is nothing like the old multilevel marketing (MLM) models. The two models are as different as night and day. The old-line firms were built on the back of a few products that were easy to copy and open to stiff competition.

> **Quixtar's model is based on sound, futuristic business criteria.**
>
> **Product choice, home delivery, and other value added concepts are all perfect for the Web.**

Worse, product often had to be inventoried by the IBOs, distributors or reps who stored them in their garage – if you can believe!

It was a true "mom and pop" shop where buyers went to pick up their orders. It worked in its day, but that day has long gone. Today's savvy shopper will never shop that way; they want to shop online and have stuff delivered.

With online ordering and "Ditto Delivery" at its core, Quixtar's model is based on sound and futuristic business criteria. Product choice, home delivery, and other value-added concepts are all perfect for the Web.

Highly-Effective, Record-Breaking Website

Quixtar was late to the Webolution. But when it showed up, it made a grand entrance and never looked back.

When launched in 1999, Quixtar's website was as big as that of General Motors. During the first 24 hours, the site was overwhelmed by 20 million hits from people wanting to shop there. That was just the beginning.

- **Within 2 weeks, Quixtar was the 5th-ranked global shopping site,** logging 52 million page views and racking up its first $1-million sales day.

- **Within 100 days, Quixtar's sales topped $100 million** and the website was selling $2 million worth of product daily.

- **After 200 days, sales topped $250 million** and it wasn't long before Quixtar kept recording peak sales days of $4 million, then $5 million, $6 million, $7 million, $8 million, $9 million.

This record-breaking streak continued into 2003, with a $10.5 million sales day.

Quixtar thus quickly became a big winner, turning into one of the Internet's top e-commerce businesses – all without spending a dime on advertising!

By September 2000, the National Retail Federation's *Stores* magazine ranked Quixtar the 7th e-commerce website – using what Quixtar says was a *low* sales estimate.

Quixtar's climb up the website rankings didn't stop there. A study by Deloitte & Touche, the big global audit firm, ranked Quixtar the No.2 retail website in Canada, topped only by Sears.com.

Then *Business 2.0* ranked Quixtar No.1 in the health and beauty category and Harris Interactive estimated Quixtar had 22% of all online sales in that category, way ahead of its lagging competitors Avon and Mary Kay.

In late 2001, *Inter@ctive Week* magazine ranked Quixtar as 2nd only to Amazon (and way ahead of eBay) in all online retail sales.

In *Future Consumer.Com*, since 1999 I've consistently forecast Quixtar in the "top 5" online retail websites of 2010. You can see why I'm very comfortable with that.

> *Inter@ctive Week* **magazine ranked Quixtar as 2nd only to Amazon (and way ahead of eBay) in all online retail sales in 2001.**

Quixtar continues to rank highly in all product categories and in overall sales and sales growth, going from strength to strength as more people shop online.

As to Quixtar's website, it's a personalized shopping portal that is functional, fun, and easy to use, with ready "help" features such as FAQs (frequently asked questions) and tip sheets of all kinds.

Tech-Savvy Positioning ...

Draws Future-Savvy Shoppers

Quixtar's website is clean and zesty, with lots of lifestyle appeal for the modern consumer.

It appeals to young consumers because it doesn't so much sell products as a new lifestyle – a Web Lifestyle. And it offers the chance to be a business owner rather than work for monolithic corporations for 40 years.

Quixtar also is attracting successful people from the big business world who have the ambition to be an independent business owner.

Quixtar thus reaches tech-savvy prosumers who can participate on one of three levels: Client, Member, or Independent Business Owner (IBO).

- **CLIENT:**
  Change your shopping habits to just be a regular online shopper; enjoy the products, time-saving convenience and shopping experience that Quixtar offers.

- **MEMBER:**
  For a nominal fee, Members get extra savings through discount pricing and membership perks.

- **INDEPENDENT BUSINESS OWNER (IBO):**
  If you are going to change your shopping habits and join the online world, **this really is the only way to go.** If you are going to be a Client or a Member and shop at Quixtar, why the heck not build your own online business in the process?

High-Touch Mentorship + High-Tech Tools

Like any good sales and marketing business, Quixtar organizations have strong human skills development programs for IBOs, based on "high-touch" mentorship teaching and "high-tech" resource tools.

- **MENTORSHIP TEACHING ("High-Touch"):**

    Mentorship is provided by those who've already built an extremely profitable business. It's an "experienced-hands-on" process.

    The current business leaders in any affiliate marketing organization have a vested and on-going interest in the business and financial success of every new IBO they register. This is totally unlike the so-called mentorship that might come from bosses in traditional businesses, most of whom only care about their own career success.

    By contrast, with Quixtar you can learn much from successful business leaders who know what works and what doesn't, thus avoiding natural mistakes and saving lots of time and trouble in building your business.

    The people who make the most money in affiliate marketing are those who spend time developing those they register. As a new IBO, it makes the utmost sense to make use of their knowledge!

- **RESOURCE TOOLS (High-Tech):**

    The high-tech toolkit includes a variety of valuable books, tapes, videos and CDs, plus high-touch seminars and conferences.

As you master these tools, they become your business-building support materials that will give your presentations professional credibility and leave a lasting impression.

All learning is about investing in yourself and your business. It boosts your self-confidence and your business-building ability.

This blended "high-tech + high-touch" program educates and motivates IBOs. It helps them grow professionally and personally, learning while they earn and build or – as Marshall McLuhan described "work" in the Internet age – while they "learn a living."

One-to-One "High-Touch" Relationships

Quixtar's "high-tech" website and business-building system uses customer relationship technology to help maintain the trademark "high-touch" customer interaction provided by super-enthusiastic IBOs.

Smart IBOs build their networks *offline*, channel their sales *online*, and manage their e-business both online *and* offline. Quixtar's success thus stems mainly from a breed of IBOs who understand how to build "high-tech + high-touch" communities of customers.

They know that online success requires one-to-one, people-oriented, long-term customer relationship building – plus cooperative teamwork and mentorship among IBOs.

Quixtar's high-touch IBOs are the key differentiator that will lead it to success over most brick-and-mortar, pure online, and hybrid retail competitors.

Nobody *outside* of network or affiliate marketing incorporates this essential "human element" into their marketing strategies.

Amazon, for example, can customize and personalize its website all it wants, but it still doesn't have human beings with whom you can interact and from whom you can learn how to succeed at growing a business.

Wal-Mart, the planet's largest retailer, may have greeters to hand you a shopping cart, but that's as high-touch as it gets. And shopping in a sterile, cavernous, big-box warehouse like Costco or Sam's is neither high-tech nor high-touch.

By contrast, the high-touch enthusiasm of Quixtar's IBOs to tap into the high-tech Web – leveraging their success to its phenomenal growth path – is creating a new 21st-century American cyber dream.

And it is a dream to which tens of millions will eventually aspire.

Solar-Powered Quixtar

To wrap up this chapter, let's recall that e-commerce markets tend to evolve into winner-take-all markets.

Networked markets tend to enable a single business to gain an overwhelmingly dominant position over time, pre-empting new entrants and thwarting competition.

In a "winner-take-all" online world, being No.1 in a product category will be awesome. Being No.2 will be very good. Beyond that, the chances of success are dubious.

In affiliate marketing, Quixtar is far and away the leader – not only in most categories but overall – and is running faster than its competitors.

While it is difficult to forecast which websites will win out in some categories, those companies blessed with a big first-mover advantage, a great brand, or much capital and human talent, will dominate.

It now seems almost certain that Quixtar will be the top online affiliate marketer and one of a handful of top online retailers – if not "king" of the entire online shopping world.

After all, with the retailing shakeout – online and offline – we've merely witnessed the "big bang" of the Web. As the e-shopping cosmos evolves and the stardust settles, we'll find a few big winners who will join the ranks of the world's premier 21st-century retailers.

> **It now seems almost certain that Quixtar will be the top online affiliate marketer and one of a handful of top online retailers – if not "king" of the entire online shopping world.**

And I believe that Quixtar has an outstanding chance to be the "sun" of that entire universe – a sun that will shine brightly and bring abundant life to all who come under its brilliant rays.

The Future QUIXTAR Consumer

7

THE SUCCESSFUL
e-BUSINESS BUILDER
High-Tech + High-Touch

O NLINE MARKETERS NEED TO RETHINK their business strategies and reposition themselves online using the "6 Ps of e-Marketing."

This is exactly what Quixtar has done – and it's working magnificently. But IBOs constantly need to review and refocus their own business marketing strategies.

The "6-Ps of e-Marketing"

My 1993 book *The Future Consumer* forecast how the Web would transform the "4 Ps" of marketing into a "New 4 Ps" *(shown in the first two columns of the following table).*

Old 4 Ps	New 4 Ps	New 6 Ps
Product	Mass-Customized Product	Mass-Customized Product
Place	AnyTime + AnyPlace	AnyTime + AnyPlace
Price	Total Value Price	Dynamic Value Price
Promotion	Precise (1:1) Positioning	Precise (1:1) Positioning
–	–	Personalized Service
–	–	Profound Experience

The Webolution proves the "New 4 Ps" model is valid. But price needs modifying, and we need two more "Ps."

• **Value Pricing**

The Web intensifies competition, often changing prices dynamically. So while "Total Value Price" is still a valid part of the mix, it really should be seen as "*Dynamic* Value Price" because value may change rapidly.

> **Savvy IBOs focus on *making* money by buying their own products – not on clipping coupons and chasing false bargains.**

Let me also stress again how value pricing is critical to understanding the Quixtar business.

As I said, many consumers are brainwashed to mistakenly chase false bargains. Conversely, prosumer IBOs must focus not on price but high-value products that drive Point Value (PV) on what they and their team buys to generate income.

– 94 –

Savvy **IBOs** focus on *making* money by buying their own products – not on clipping coupons and chasing false bargains.

You don't own a Quixtar business to *save* money but to *make* money – money you can then *truly* save for your future.

• Two Additional "Ps"

The online marketing mix also needs 2 extra "Ps," creating a "New 6 Ps" model *(third column in the table).*

"High-touch" service is paramount in managing customer relations in a "high-tech" world. So we need the fifth "P" of **"Personalized Service"** to close the loop with mass-customized product. Indeed, customization and personalization overlay all parts of the e-marketing mix.

Finally, an over-arching goal of online marketing is to persuade the customer to bookmark your website as one of their favorites to which they will readily and repeatedly return to buy more products.

User "experience" of a website is much more critical than product packaging, product display, or advertising. Hence, we need to add the sixth "P" of **"Profound Experience."**

As discussed in Chapter 6, these "6 Ps" are the 6 keys to Quixtar's successful business model.

> **You don't own a Quixtar business to *save* money but to *make* money – money you can then *truly* save for your future.**

Relating the Product to the Customer

These "6 Ps" also form two logical clusters, as follows:

- **The first three "Ps" are Product-Related**
- **The last three "Ps" are Customer-Related**

• 3 PRODUCT-RELATED HIGH-TECH "Ps"

The first three, product-related "Ps" need no explanation. Successful retailers carry minimum inventory as manufacturing shifts from mass production to mass customization.

As more customers configure more products for themselves online, point-and-click prefabrication of everyday items, zapped to robotized factories and delivered direct to homes, will be commonplace.

As shown by Dell or Amazon.com – and Quixtar – these aspects can be highly-automated activities that a manufacturer and/or retailer conducts routinely, at low fixed and variable cost.

The main point is to recognize that the old linear supply chain is a defunct concept.

Mass-customized products, e-channels, and dynamic pricing become interwoven into a "value web" that must function flawlessly and seamlessly in real time.

It must be a truly friction-free interdependent network that customers can take for granted as a reliable part of their daily routine.

Quixtar's "Ditto Delivery" model personifies this client-focused "value web" concept.

• 3 CUSTOMER-RELATED HIGH-TOUCH "Ps"

Because the high-tech "Ditto Delivery" process is automatic and operates smoothly, Quixtar and its IBOs will be able to devote more attention to the three, customer-related "Ps".

Indeed, because the Web amplifies word-of-mouth through word-of-modem, online marketers must allocate most resources to building profound customer experiences.

To optimize customer experience, much time and money must be invested in database marketing, customer relationship management (CRM), and website design – design that doesn't just create a website but builds a meaningful, distinctive, compelling online presence.

> IBOs, at every level, must spare no effort to build customer relationships that ensure complete satisfaction at all times.

The goal is speedy, personalized, relationships that accumulate repeat sales.

People return to such sites 6 times more often than other sites, spend more time on the site, buy more items, and spend more money.

And time and money spent also increase as they visit the website more frequently.

By implication, IBOs at every level must spare no effort to build customer relationships that ensure complete satisfaction at all times – whether the customer is a Client, a Member, or an IBO teammate.

The Online Shopping "Experience"

Satisfaction is critical because the Web disconnects shopping from physical location.

The old maxim of "location, location, location" now becomes location-less e-tailing: a website, a delivery system, a business building process, and a personal relationship.

This converges or blurs the lines between advertising, marketing and sales, which can't be separate functions.

As Quixtar shows, you don't need to advertise. Instead, the objective now is to focus on what each customer experiences with the e-brand.

Marketing and sales also must occur in real time. Monthly or quarterly campaigns – and aggregate sales reports – are useless.

Each customer is a "market of one" and the "campaign" with each customer must be adjusted "on the fly" in response to each sale transaction.

Most important is the lifetime value of a customer's business *(discussed later)*. Again, therefore, Client, Member, and IBO relationships are primary.

> **Consumers are as individual as their fingerprints, and the Web is empowering personalized consumption.**

Quixtar harnesses the Web's power to ship direct and to track data on what people buy. This helps IBOs manage and build their own business *(again discussed later)*.

From "Mass" Advertising ...
to "One-to-One" Relationships

The main point here is that the Webolution smashes the era of "mass" to smithereens. Consumers are as individual as their fingerprints, and the Web is empowering personalized consumption.

In the Agricultural Age, there was no advertising. Marketing was local and based on *personal* consumer tastes and buying patterns. The Industrial Age brought the *impersonal* world of mass production, mass consumption and mass advertising.

But the Webolution changes all that. **Individual buyers are again reachable on a personal basis.**

And tech-savvy buyers expect to be fully informed about product benefits, and their search for value is best satisfied through product information and strong customer relationships.

Sales pitches and hype are counter-productive. Buyers simply insist on making up their own minds.

Consider just two "reversals" the Web brings to the advertising, marketing, and sales process:

> • **ADVERTISING "PUSH":** Traditional advertising tells a mass consumer audience that a specific product exists and sells its benefits. Consumers indirectly pay for the cost of those ads through the cost of products that are "pushed" through the distribution chain – products which they are then "pushed" to buy by advertisers and retail store clerks.

- **DEMAND "PULL":** By contrast, Quixtar links individual buyers to a virtual showroom, giving them enough personally-relevant information to help them make their own purchase decisions across a whole range of products, not just one product. Quixtar "prosumers" thus buy products that contain no advertising costs because they buy direct; and each product sells itself through demand "pull." Moreover, IBOs are motivated to buy, thanks to the bonuses and incentives they receive to build their own business.

In fact, the Web is the *only* medium where the user can see a product, inquire about it quickly and in detail, compare prices, and then decide to buy – then and there online – and save time and money doing it.

Word-of-mouth was the most effective product endorsement in the pre-industrial, "oral" society. However, **word-of-modem** is the most effective "mode" of product endorsement in the Web Age. It spreads rapidly and replicates exponentially and organically, similar to this diagram:

oOo

oOo oOo

oOo oOo oOo

oOo oOo oOo oOo oOo

oOo oOo oOo oOo oOo oOo oOo oOo

oOo oOo oOo oOo oOo oOo oOo oOo oOo oOo oOo oOo oOo

(This particular Network Growth Effect is based on the Fibonacci sequence: 1-2-3-5-8-13-etc.)

The network growth effect not only brings in new shoppers. It also builds sales much faster than in a non-Web business.

As a result, the Web will be dominated by a handful of major e-tailers such as Quixtar, Amazon, and eBay.

On the Web, marketing thus is much more a matter of one-to-one interaction, not selling.

IBOs don't "sell" anything; they show others how to change their shopping habits. They are in the Web Lifestyle business.

They promote online shopping as part of a "Web Life." That's it!

This is a big shift: from the old-fashioned "in-your-face" pitch to a modern "get a Web Life" approach.

> **IBOs don't "sell" anything.**
>
> **They show others how to change their shopping habits.**
>
> **They are in the Web Lifestyle business.**
>
> **They promote online shopping as part of a "Web Life."**
>
> **That's it!**

High-Tech + High-Touch Business Culture

Just as the Web demands high-tech/high-touch methods, business cultures also need to become high-tech and high-touch, in at least two ways:

- **By redefining the nature of the business; and**
- **By bonding with customers.**

The Future QUIXTAR Consumer

• REDEFINE THE NATURE OF THE BUSINESS ...

as a "High-Tech" Information-Based Business

The Web restructures each industry and redefines the very nature of business. For example, the financial service sector is no longer in the "money business" but the business of "information *about* money."

Affiliate marketers are in the business of "info *about* products." They never actually see the products which, in Quixtar's case, are shipped direct to the customer.

This allows IBOs to manage and drive the growth of their business by studying reports on who is ordering which products and which of their team members are truly building a business *(see later)*.

• BOND THE CUSTOMERS ...

with "High-Touch" Personalized Relationships

Business ever was and always will be a people-to-people endeavor. Success online will be greatly enhanced by those who bring human relationships to the fore.

Competitors can copy products, match prices, and use similar channels – including websites and automatic product delivery. But they will *never* duplicate that very special personal bond that Quixtar has with its best customers through its IBOs.

Managing IBO and customer relationships in a "high-touch" way doesn't just build bonds; it fortifies them with loyalty and trust. In turn, trust leads to more information sharing – and more profitable transactions.

– 102 –

Building "Share of Customer"

Companies that embrace "high-tech + high-touch" will win the digital race because they will be best at building "share of customer."

Old-time marketers – and old-time IBOs – tend to focus on one-time sales and tot up what everybody bought *last* month. E-business builders focus on the future *lifetime* earnings stream coming from each customer.

Futuristic IBOs focus on building *tomorrow's* "share of customer," not *yesterday's* "share of market" – on *tomorrow's* PV (point value), not *yesterday's* PV.

Few businesses ever consider how much a loyal, satisfied customer is worth. Online, you can't afford not to do so; indeed, it becomes easy to do so.

Clearly, the expected lifetime value of a customer – that is, the amount of net profit a business might expect to earn on the *repeat* sale of products to that customer *over their lifetime* – depends on their buying power.

Astute IBOs model the lifetime value of similar customers and then, based on an individual customer's buying behavior, forecast that customer's lifetime value to the business.

Obviously, this profile differs for each product, some of which are bought less frequently.

> **Focus on the future *lifetime* earnings stream coming from each customer.**
>
> **Build *tomorrow's* PV not *yesterday's* PV.**

Astute **IBOs realize that it costs virtually *nothing* to retain an existing customer by ensuring their ongoing satisfaction. It requires *much* time, effort, and money to replace a lost customer.**

Smart IBOs thus focus much effort on customer retention. They also realize what repeat sales are truly worth, especially on mundane everyday products.

For example, if a person spends $10 a week on cleaning products, then over 50 years of adult life they spend $26,000 – just on that one product!

> **Lifetime value is the clear-as-day advantage of having your own e-business with Quixtar because of its endless revenue flows.**

If the net profit on that product is 10% then the lifetime value of a cleaning product customer is $2,600.

Net profit on a one-time sale is only $1. Most merchants simply take that single sale for granted as part of total monthly sales.

Futuristic IBOs do their utmost to please customers on every sale.

That way, they become loyal customers for life. And that approach gives them a big edge over a traditional merchant – in the above case, a $2,599 edge!

Fortunately, IBOs are motivated to generate repeat sales because they earn ongoing revenue on those sales. There's the difference: store clerks don't earn anything as a reward for generating repeat business.

So lifetime value is the clear-as-day advantage of having your own Quixtar business because of its endless revenue flows.

Starting Your Own e-Business

Due to the ongoing shift to online shopping – and the on-going income benefits it offers "prosumers" – millions of families will be attracted to it.

To achieve truly independent financial freedom for themselves – as well as for their children and grand-children – futuristic families thus will leverage their wealth to Quixtar.

Many of these Quixtar businesses will make their members rich beyond imagination.

For example, in 2003 Quixtar created twice as many *brand new* Diamonds as were created in 2002. And all the other "pin" levels saw similarly high growth rates.

> To achieve truly-independent financial freedom for themselves – as well as for their children and their grandchildren – futuristic families will leverage their wealth to the Web via Quixtar.

As Quixtar continues to expand, inevitably there will be many more people at every level of success. **It's almost a mathematical certainty!**

Build Your Dream, Not Somebody Else's

Economic success comes to people in a variety of ways. For most people, it has been through "blood, sweat, and tears" – working for somebody else.

Every day, millions of otherwise intelligent people are forced out of their homes to "commute" – a social disaster most would prefer to avoid. (See my book *Future Living* for a hilarious description of this idiocy.)

Let's face it; you rarely can become wealthy when working for somebody else. Think about it: most well-off people own a business. They write their own paycheck.

So quit the rat rate, stop building someone else's dream, and start building your own!

The prosumer boom is leading this wealth-building trend. And you either want to be part of it or you don't.

In fact, we could see the first billionaire of the "prosumer" network economy by 2010. And I'll lay you odds that he/she will do it through a Quixtar business.

What Kind of Business is Best for You?

Of those who already own home businesses, 81% say they like the freedom and having control over their own destiny. And a whopping 93% say they have no regrets.

Why not find a profitable opportunity that suits *your* true life goals and motivations?

As fully examined in *Future Consumer.com*, you have four main options, as follows:

1. **Be Self-Employed:** Your own niche business.
2. **Be an Affiliate:** Of an e-business like Amazon.
3. **Be a Franchisee:** With a chain-store franchisor.
4. **Be an Independent Business Owner (or IBO):** A form of "private franchising" in a network or affiliate marketer such as Quixtar.

As concluded in *Future Consumer.com*, a Quixtar IBO business is by far the _best_ home-based opportunity for the vast majority of people.

The benefits are too numerous to list.

It needs little or no capital, you can decide how much time to invest, and yet you have a duplicable franchise-like business that you can grow. Running such an e-business is not onerous. You have no employees to manage or pay, no inventory, and no office overhead – in fact the cost of your home office may be a tax deduction, as may some other expenses.

Now, while start-up costs are trifling, treat your Quixtar business like a million-dollar business because that's what it has the potential to become!

Each day, online marketers sell millions of dollars worth of vitamins, beauty items, cleaning products, and many other in-demand consumables.

> **Treat your Quixtar business like a million-dollar business because that's what it has the potential to become!**

In 2003, Quixtar *averaged* $3 million a day in sales, 7-days-a-week, throughout the year – its best day was $10.5 million! – and racked up $1.1 billion overall.

Capturing the "Prosumer" Trend

Quixtar is the clear leader in online network marketing. Other big names such as Avon or Herbalife are playing catch up and lagging behind. Most others are not worth joining. But the big ones offer huge opportunities to those who commit their futures to them.

> **When you join a select network like Quixtar, you determine your own income by your efforts, skill, and desire.**
>
> **You become your own boss.**

When you join a select network team like Quixtar, you determine your own income by your efforts, skill, and desire. You become your own boss, work when you want, and with whom you choose.

Obviously, the more time you commit and the faster you learn the business, then the faster you will grow your sales and your income will multiply.

In terms of annual profit, a 2002 government survey found that most home-based businesses *gross* between $125,000 and $650,000 a year. The average *net* profit of an individually-owned affiliate business (across the entire industry, not just Quixtar) is about $64,000 – double the average workplace salary.

A big company such as Quixtar generally yields more income, depending on its compensation plan and bonus structure. And in 2003, Quixtar paid out extra growth incentive bonuses to drive the business even faster.

The biggest bonus of all, of course is that you get to spend more time at home with your spouse and children and can become more involved in their lives.

Leveraging Network Economics

If you go the affiliate marketing route, you need to leverage the network effect that will grow your business.

Affiliate marketing in particular has the potential to grow exponentially in line with "Metcalfe's Law" of network expansion.

As explained earlier, a network grows inexorably because, as it expands, its value increases for all its members. It thus attracts still more members and grows to the mutual benefit of everybody in the network.

While it isn't a franchisor like McDonald's, Quixtar is a network of essentially "privately-franchised" individuals. These IBO business builders register new people to further grow their own sales network *and* the larger main network of which they are a part.

They "duplicate" themselves through others by sponsoring or "franchising" them into Quixtar and teaching them how to build a business of their own. In turn, they earn a commission on their subsequent sales.

Thus, in affiliate marketing, everybody wins as the network grows. Recall, for example, how Quixtar's bonus payout grew from $143 million in 2000 to $334 million in 2003, as its network grew. That's the power of online prosumer marketing.

Growing a Network Business

There are two main challenges in growing such a business:

1. Registering others; and

2. Driving and managing growth.

1. REGISTERING OTHERS

Since 1999, I have dialogued at length about the Quixtar business with scores of IBOs – from Crown Ambassadors to the latest newbie IBO.

From those discussions, it's abundantly evident that there is no point in willy-nilly registering people into your business who simply aren't suited or are nowhere near ready for e-shopping. That results in dropouts that diminish the very "network growth effect" you're trying to leverage.

So what kind of people should you register?

To answer that question, you need to think like a talent scout, not a recruiter!

You are looking, of course, either for Clients, Members, or IBOs. You need to mentally categorize people as such, as you listen to their needs, aspirations and motivations, and as you assess their talents.

So be patient, diligent, and selective in building your business team. You are looking for a range of qualified and talented people – Clients, Members, and IBOs – who you can then coach to team-building success.

Do it right the first time! Don't think everybody you bump into is ready for your team.

After all, it takes more time to *rebuild* a business than to build it properly from the outset.

Handpick your talent and spend your time coaching the gung-ho prospects – people who really have what it takes to build a successful, fast-growth prosumer business, just like you do.

> **Do it right the first time!**
>
> **Think like a talent scout, not a recruiter!**
>
> **Be patient, diligent, and selective in building your business team.**
>
> **Spend your time coaching the gung-ho prospects.**

• **Spotting Future IBOs:** In terms of registering new IBOs, then, my rule of thumb would be to mentally consider the following two questions:

(1) **"If this were my very own stand-alone business, with salaried employees that I pay, would I hire this person and pay them $25,000-$50,000 a year out of my own pocket to be a sales or business development person?"**

(2) "Is this person a team player who wants to learn the business and who can be coached to a higher level?"

If the answers are "Yes" then you've found a winning IBO team member.

If the answers are "No" then I'd carefully weigh how much time you are going to spend trying to register that person as an IBO. That person may well turn out to be a super IBO, but will more likely be a better consumer than a prosumer. I'd sign them up as a Client or a Member.

• **Future Clients or Members:** Since yours is an online shopping business, you also need to pre-qualify Clients and Members (and IBOs, of course) accordingly.

If you want people to change their habits to shop online, and to start buying from the get go, then they must have a Web access device, already be online, and preferably have bought something online at least once. In short, they know what the Web and online shopping are all about.

If they are Web-savvy, then "Bingo," you've at least got a Client or a Member, and maybe a good IBO.

The point is that you don't want to be training people how to buy a PC, how to use it, how to surf, or how to shop online. People who can't do that yet aren't ready for e-commerce.

You need people who at least are starting out on the Web "learning curve." In short:

Let AOL, Amazon, and eBay train your prospects for you – then register them!

2. DRIVING and MANAGING GROWTH

To grow any business you need to set goals. Quixtar IBOs need to set goals to grow their PV (Point Value of products bought, on which bonuses are paid). PV has to be driven and managed.

Fortunately *(as we saw in Chapter 6)*, the "Ditto Delivery" system is designed to allow you to project your PV volume and that of your IBO team as a whole. Use it to drive and manage the growth of your business.

• Driving PV

You need to *drive* PV to really make it happen for you. In setting goals, however, do not overshoot or undershoot in setting Point Value targets.

If you set unrealistically high PV goals and fail to meet them, your team will lose heart. Set PV goals too low, and you'll fall behind and also lose heart.

In 2003, e-shopping grew by at least 20% over 2002 in Canada and the United States. While the growth rate will fluctuate, to leverage the "network growth effect" you need to keep growing at the overall market rate or better, just to keep up. In fact, in regions where growth is faster, you need to grow faster than national online sales – and faster than the Quixtar growth rate – to keep pace.

In setting your overall Point Value target, you also need to set individual PV targets – for each of your IBOs *and* for each Member and Client – so that, in total, you will meet your overall business PV growth objective.

• Managing PV

Then you need to *manage* your business against those Point Value targets by analyzing sales reports at least weekly, if not daily.

Remember, this is an information-driven Internet business; you manage it through the power of networked information. Use real-time PV (not just last month's PV) to drive growth over the long term.

PV trends will reveal which of your IBOs need help now, not yesterday. You can also use the PV data to cross-sell and up-sell both the prosumers and consumers in your business that are falling short.

If sales fall behind and you fail to address it, then you will not catch up and will fail to meet your overall target for the year. Bonus checks will decline and disenchanted people will leave the business.

Conversely, if you get most of your team members ahead of target on a cumulative weekly basis, then you will be far more likely to exceed your goals and to keep everybody motivated. In turn, bonus checks will rise and drop-outs will be few and far between. Indeed, IBOs will be motivated to register more people.

In doing all this, remember that your best customer is you!

You should switch as many of your *own* shopping dollars as possible to *your* Quixtar business. Truly get to know the products and their benefits – not just their PV – and be loyal to them. Then you are in a great position to convince other team members to do likewise.

And PV will climb faster than you might imagine.

Climbing the Quixtar "Escalator"™

Building a Quixtar business can be viewed like climbing a long escalator. The Quixtar "Escalator" has 100 steps.

It looks a bit like this unique Japanese escalator, which rises in stages, with a short, moving mezzanine between each stage.

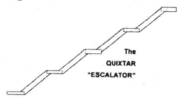

Each stage represents the incremental progress in reaching a new "pin" level of success.

Envision it rising to key "pin" levels at each mezzanine: Platinum, then Ruby, Sapphire, Emerald, and Diamond.

Build more "Escalators" and you will go EDC, Double Diamond, Triple Diamond, Crown, and on to Crown Ambassador.

Of course you can't stand still on the "Escalator" and get a "free ride." Stand still for too long and you'll stumble backward and fall down.

To successfully ascend the "Escalator" you must methodically climb the steps by determinedly driving sales to higher and higher PV levels – and by helping your team of IBOs to do the same.

Indeed, for your "Escalator" to rise, you have to help your IBOs build *their* businesses by helping them bring *new* IBOs onto the first step of the "Escalator."

You have to climb the Quixtar "Escalator" together. You build *your* franchise by in fact building the businesses of those new IBOs you register. And the faster you grow *their* business, growing sales for *them*, the more rapidly they *and* you will achieve higher success levels.

Just as you can't get a "free ride" up, neither can you relax at a major success-level mezzanine. Rest on your laurels and you likely will not re-qualify and, again, your business will fall back down.

The success-level mezzanine is where you consolidate your business width and depth and mobilize your team for the next ascent.

Climb the Quixtar "Escalator" conscientiously and deliberately in this fashion and, with this book in hand, I virtually guarantee you will succeed.

The Bottom Line

This book has explained how the Webolution is dramatically reshaping life, business, and shopping.

Please consider its findings as they apply to your situation, as follows:

• IF YOU ARE A CONSUMER

Consider how you can save oodles of time by changing your shopping habits – by simply switching your spending from supermarkets and big box warehouse stores – to buy online as a Quixtar Member or Client.

- **IF YOU ARE A PROSPECTIVE QUIXTAR IBO**

  Consider how affiliate marketing will help you achieve your dreams, not only by earning a commission on everything you and your team will buy from Quixtar, but by owning your own turnkey IBO business. And commit to build that business with your sponsor's help.

- **IF YOU ALREADY ARE A QUIXTAR IBO**

  Review how you conduct and go about building your business to see how some of the trends and ideas discussed in this book might help you be more successful. In particular, focus on future lifetime PV value and commit to driving your business up the Quixtar "Escalator."

In conclusion, just let me re-iterate how strongly I believe that the Quixtar I-commerce business model is perfectly aligned with the forces of the Webolution.

When you join Quixtar's winning team you give yourself the best possible e-business opportunity.

Look at these Quixtar facts:

- **Easily the #1 affiliate marketing company.**
- **The first network marketer to go online.**
- **Profitable from day one.**
- **Way ahead of its closest competitors.**
- **Blew past $1 billion in annual sales in 2003.**
- **2nd only to Amazon in *all* of online retailing.**
- **Paid out $1 billion in commissions in 4 years.**

As I said at the outset, *"Quixtar was destined to be big."* It *is* big! And it is getting bigger and more successful.

I am fully confident that it will meet my forecast to be one of the "Top 5" online shopping websites of 2010. Indeed, it could turn out to be No.1 well before then.

Whether that happens, of course, is in your hands. But I believe in you! And wish you a super-fantastic future!

Frank Feather

P.S.

I very much welcome ideas and suggestions on how this book might be improved to serve you even better.

Please send your ideas to FutureTrends2020@aol.com and you *will* receive a personal, and grateful, reply.

Of course, should any of my views conflict with those of your Quixtar organization, please tell me about them also.

Meanwhile, please take my ideas under advisement and heed those of your sponsors.

Thank you again!

TO CONTACT FRANK FEATHER
About Speaking Engagements

E-Mail: FutureTrends2020@aol.com

Phone: **(905) 642-9090**

ABOUT FRANK FEATHER

F RANK FEATHER is a global business and Web
futurist and best-selling author who uses a unique
trend tracking and forecasting system.

He is totally independent of Quixtar *(see below).*

1. BIOGRAPHICAL DATA

**Frank Feather is a strategy consultant to global companies,
international organizations, and national governments.**

He is President and founder of his own consulting companies:
Future-Trends.Com and **Glocal Marketing Consultants.**

Frank has been called "a walking encyclopedia on the future." In
fact, in 1996, McMillan's *Encyclopedia on the Future* put him
among the **"Top 100 Futurists of All Time"** – a list that
included Leonardo da Vinci.

He is a former planning and marketing executive with three of
the world's largest banks (Barclays, TD, and CIBC). In 1979
Frank coined the now well-known phrase **"Thinking Globally,
Acting Locally"** and then developed the related concept of
"glocal" (global + local) marketing. In 1980, he was Chairman &
Secretary General of the **First Global Conference on the
Future**, an event with 6,000 delegates from 56 countries and still
the largest conference on the future ever held.

He has advised an A-Z of global corporations – names such as
AT&T, IBM, Ford, GM, Nokia, and Shell. He also has consulted
to the World Bank/IMF, the UN, and the governments of

Canada, Mexico and the United States. And he's been a Special Advisor to China on economic and market reform since 1984.

He is the author (or editor) of several best-selling books:

- **G-FORCES: The 35 Global Forces Restructuring Our Future** (1989)
- **OPTIMISTIC OUTLOOKS** (co-editor, 1982)
- **THINKING GLOBALLY, ACTING LOCALLY** (editor, 1980)
- **THE FUTURE CONSUMER** (1993 and 1997)
- **FUTURE CONSUMER.COM: The Webolution of Shopping to 2010** (2000, 2nd edition 2002)
- **THE FUTURE QUIXTAR CONSUMER** (2002, 2003, 2004)
- **FUTURE LIVING: 9 Steps to a Better Life in an Uncertain World** (2003)
- **GET A WEB LIFE** (2004)

In great demand on the international lecture circuit, Frank speaks to business and association events of all kinds across all industries.

Frank holds a BA (Honors Admin) from York University (Toronto), did MBA graduate studies there, and taught MBA courses there. He holds qualifications from the U.K. and Canadian Institutes of Bankers, was awarded a PMgr designation by the Canadian Institute of Management, and is a Fellow of the American Association for Social Psychiatry.

A proud native of Yorkshire, Frank says he is "frank by name and nature." Down to earth and forthright, he speaks his mind and injects an uncommon amount of common sense into solidly-researched yet far-reaching writing and provocative speeches.

Frank is married to Tammie Min Tan, a native of Shanghai, and they have two adopted daughters from China, Melissa and Ashley. Their home lies amid a forested community on the outskirts of Toronto, Canada, where they live a Web Lifestyle.

2. VIEWPOINT INDEPENDENT OF QUIXTAR

Frank Feather is an "outsider" to Quixtar, with no conflict of interest in writing this book.

Neither he nor any member of his family has any direct business relationship with the Quixtar Corporation.

As an outside guest speaker, on occasion he is privileged to address Quixtar meetings, for which he receives a typical public speaking honorarium. Some events are taped with his permission, but he receives no royalty or income from such recordings.

As well, in 2000, he was invited by Quixtar via his lecture agent to appear in a corporate video called *Quixtar: It's Your Future – Go There!* He received a typical one-time speaker's honorarium but earns no royalties from that video.

In all such situations, the opinions he expresses are entirely his own.

3. RESEARCH METHODOLOGY

Frank Feather uses several empirical "content analysis" and "trend monitoring" techniques.

1. **Internet Content Analysis Program (ICAP):** In 1997, the author commissioned this proprietary software package to conduct "computerized content analysis" of the Internet, via the Internet. Content analysis is a technique used by the CIA and other intelligence organs. The author believes ICAP is the most sophisticated futures research methodology in use outside the CIA.

2. **Netrends Smart Agents:** In conjunction with ICAP, several "Netrends Smart Agents" constantly roam the Internet, e-mailing their results into a database where they are automatically sorted, ranked, and then analyzed by ICAP.

3. **Delphi Study:** Extensive Delphi studies are conducted via the Internet to develop a scenario on the future of the Internet and various e-commerce sectors. Participants are 130+ key thought leaders, executives, and industry analysts.

4. **2,600 Web Sites Evaluated:** Based on a composite of criteria used by web design experts, 2,600+ web sites are constantly evaluated on a multi-element "Web Lifestyle" matrix.

5. **Webographics:** Consumers are evaluated using a variety of "webographic"™ variables.

4. <u>FORECASTING ONLINE SALES</u>

The volume of future e-tail sales can be predicted by forecasting five variables, which compound on each other:

      1. How many people will use the Internet?
      2. What percentage of them will buy online?
      3. How much will they spend and how frequently?
      4. On what items will they spend it?
      5. At which Web sites will they spend it?

To answer these five questions, each variable is forecast by complex computer models.

INDEX

Advertising 25, 63, 99-100
Amazon.com 20, 25, 52, 64-65, 86, 90, 96, 112, 117

Cell Phones 10, 14, 15, 17, 18, 36, 49, 53, 59, 60
Computers 9, 11, 13, 14, 27, 29, 32, 34, 38, 52, 59, 60
Consumer Segments 58-60 (and throughout the book)
Customer Lifetime Value 103-105

"Ditto Delivery" 74, 76-81, 97

eBay 25, 28, 65, 86, 112
Economic Webolution 19-31

Family 25-26, 28-29, 30-31, 36-39, 61
First-Mover Advantage 23-24, 48
Franchisee 107, 109
Future Consumer.Com 2, 20, 46, 69, 77, 86, 106, 107

Gates, Bill 9, 15, 33
Growing an Independent e-Business 110-116

Health & Beauty 53-55, 75
High-Tech / High-Touch 22, 88-90, 101-102
Home-Based Business / Economy 25-30, 38-39, 105-107
Hype 9, 12, 63

I-Commerce 84-85, 117
Independent Business Owners (IBOs) 81, 87, 97, 107, 116 (and throughout the book)
Industrial Revolution 26-27, 37-38, 46

Marketing / Marketing Mix 75, 93-97
McLuhan, Marshall 28, 89
Mentoring IBOs 88
Moore's Law 14, 27

"Network Growth Effect" 13, 24, 100, 109

One-to-One Marketing 5, 20, 23, 24, 64, 68, 75, 89, 99
Online "Learning Curve" 12, 64-67
Online Shopping 43-56, 57-63, 68-70 (and throughout the book)

Product Point Value (PV) 81, 113-114
Product Pricing 82, 94-95
Product Types 50-52
Prosumers (throughout the book)

QUIXTAR 71-91, 93-118 (and throughout the book)
Quixtar "Escalator" 115-116

Registering IBOs 110-112

Share of Customer 102-105
Skeptics 10, 11, 12
Social Webolution 33-41
Super-Boom 27-28
Supermarkets 40 41, 77, 79

Technical Webolution 9-17
Toffler, Alvin 22

Value Chain / Value Web 23, 94-95

Web Lifestyle 12, 23, 33-41, 87, 101
Webolution 1-41 (and throughout the book)
WebPhones 10, 15-16, 33, 40
Winner-Take-All Markets 23, 24-25, 90
Women Shoppers 25, 37, 54, 55, 60
Word-of-Modem, 64, 100
Word-of-Mouth, 64, 100

The Future QUIXTAR Consumer

NOTES